Your Personal Parenting Guide

Infant and Childcare Wisdom
from a Top Pediatrician

Charlotte E. Thompson, M.D.

Your Personal Parenting Guide: Infant and Childcare Wisdom from a Top Pediatrician

Copyright © 2015 by Atlantic Publishing Group, Inc.
1405 SW 6th Ave. • Ocala, Florida 34471 • 800-814-1132 • 352-622-1875–Fax
Website: www.atlantic-pub.com • E-mail: sales@atlantic-pub.com
SAN Number: 268-1250

Library of Congress Cataloging-in-Publication Data

Thompson, Charlotte E.
  Your personal parenting guide : infant and childcare wisdom from a top pediatrician / by Charlotte E. Thompson, M.D.
       pages cm
  Includes bibliographical references and index.
  ISBN 978-1-62023-035-0 (alk. paper) -- ISBN 1-62023-035-6 (alk. paper) 1. Parenting. 2. Parent and child. 3. Infants--Care. 4. Child care. I. Title.
  HQ755.8.T5633 2015
  649'.1--dc23
                              2015001945

Printed on Recycled Paper

Printed in the United States

Reduce. Reuse.
RECYCLE.

A decade ago, Atlantic Publishing signed the Green Press Initiative. These guidelines promote environmentally friendly practices, such as using recycled stock and vegetable-based inks, avoiding waste, choosing energy-efficient resources, and promoting a no-pulping policy. We now use 100-percent recycled stock on all our books. The results: in one year, switching to post-consumer recycled stock saved 24 mature trees, 5,000 gallons of water, the equivalent of the total energy used for one home in a year, and the equivalent of the greenhouse gases from one car driven for a year.

Over the years, we have adopted a number of dogs from rescues and shelters. First there was Bear and after he passed, Ginger and Scout. Now, we have Kira, another rescue. They have brought immense joy and love not just into our lives, but into the lives of all who met them.

We want you to know a portion of the profits of this book will be donated in Bear, Ginger and Scout's memory to local animal shelters, parks, conservation organizations, and other individuals and nonprofit organizations in need of assistance.

– Douglas & Sherri Brown,
President & Vice-President of Atlantic Publishing

To Barbara
Mel
Sean
Jennifer, Alisa, Stephanie,
Dexter and Jem
Freya and Alistair,

With Love

Table of Contents

Acknowledgments

My 50 years of experience as a pediatrician, mother, and grandmother and my knowledge of children could not have been offered to parents without the help of a special family. Thirty years ago when I practiced in San Diego, I had stopped taking new patients because my pediatric practice had become too large and busy. Despite this, Barbara Hinton persuaded me to be the pediatrician for her three girls. We had a long friendship until her death three years ago and her input for this book, as well as those of her two daughters, Alisa and Stephanie, now young mothers, made all the difference.

Parents, these days, face a somewhat scary and different world. I hope by sharing my experience and training, as well as the questions and input from the young mothers, that this book can be a great help to all parents.

I want to thank all members of the Hinton family: Barbara, Mel, Jennifer, Alisa, and Stephanie for their help, friendship, and support. Barbara asked me to add this last word that *"Parents need to remember to always do what is in the best interest of each child."*

My grandchildren, Heather and Alexander Thompson and my son, Dr. Geoffrey Thompson helped immensely with editing and computer help and I am very grateful.

The Publisher, Doug Brown, his office manager, Crystal Edwards and all those in Atlantic Publishing who helped make this book available for parents deserve my greatest thanks.

Foreword

Dr. Charlotte Thompson has written a lovely guide which shares her wise counsel. Countless parents have benefited from her assistance during her many years as a practicing pediatrician. Now all parents can read her thoughts on raising healthy, happy children.

I was first introduced to Dr. Charlotte when as a psychologist working with children in San Diego; I met a great many parents who sang her praises. They were delighted to be able to rely on her expertise, her practical suggestions, and her support. It is a pleasure to see that Dr. Charlotte's words are now in print. All parents will be able to access the information and resources needed to meet each new situation as it arises; they will have a complete guidebook, from this seasoned expert, who knows and loves children.

Dr. Charlotte not only loves and respects children; she loves, respects, and understands their parents. She has dedicated herself to the care of children and their parents for nearly 50 years. She was always there to address every concern, physical or psychological. She was always willing to go the extra mile or ten for the children and parents in her care. For many years, she had evening seminars for parents covering a wide variety of child development topics. It was my privilege to speak to one of her evening groups. I was impressed by the large turnout, the keen interest of the participants and the level of sophistication she had cultivated in the parents of her child patients. The discussion was lively and positive with her warm support.

No frightened parent or parent with an emergent concern was ever left to suffer in confusion while awaiting her return call. She was always available. Once when my granddaughter was tiny and suffering from a painful ear infection, she was the lucky recipient of her care. The local pediatrician was unable to diagnose the problem because, "the child would not let him look in her ears." Dr. Charlotte said this was unacceptable, jumped in her car, and drove 30 miles. She examined Penny's ears on the dining room table. And yes, of course, she had no trouble encouraging the child to be examined. Dr. Charlotte never met a child she could not sooth and comfort, regardless of their level of distress. Her wonderful rapport with children came in no small measure from her profound respect for children as individuals.

In this book, Dr. Charlotte gives parents the support and confidence to be their best selves. For the last half-century or more, our society has been preoccupied with the concerns of raising our children to be mentally and physically healthy, intelligent, sensitive, and successful. There was the belief that all of this rested on the parent-child interaction and parents' excellence. This has led to anxiety in every interaction and the anxiety leaves children experiencing their parents as indecisive or even unpredictable or indulgent. Worried parents have wrapped their children in cotton or become "helicopter rescuing" before the youngsters can experience problem solving and learn by doing. This book provides practical, wise, and reassuring parental guidance.

Readers will develop a sense of wellbeing and confidence and will feel comfortable about themselves as parents, even on those difficult days when we all make mistakes. Dr. Charlotte advises, "If you have lost control or been too harsh, go ahead and say, 'I'm sorry.'" No parent can always be in control and without fault". Good advice, after all children need "good enough" parents, not perfect parents, not stressed parents, not worried and anxious parents. They need parents who take time for mother-time, for father-time, and time to enjoy playing with their babies or children.

Although there are many parent advice books, few authors can bring the experience and compassion to child rearing questions that Dr. Thompson brings. In stories gleaned from her years of caring for children, she highlights all the major issues parents face day-to-day with their baby or child and provides wise and useful answers. How many times have parents wondered what to do when their infant is crying too long? The answer is in the book. Or wondered if the time is right for toilet training? Or what to expect when traveling with small children? These and many more questions are considered and illustrated with vignettes from real life.

An extremely valuable part of the book is the extensive Appendix. Helpful websites are provided, as well as toll-free numbers to access specialized information. There is an immunization schedule, charts for developmental steps, teeth development, height and weight, and chores.

Sections on important firsts and snowing/rainy day activities will be referred to often. There is also an appendix to access resources, including resources for children with special needs. The bibliography will be extremely useful to all parents.

The first section of the Appendix is however, my favorite. Dr. Thompson presents some of the many questions parents have asked, and these questions will resonate with readers and their questions. Topics such as what to do when there is a possibility of bullying at school, or when a two-year-old does not like vegetables, or when grandparents bring too many toys, her answers provide support and a plan. The question of grandparents gets special attention. Chapter 20 gives guidelines for dealing with those difficult situations, which can arise with grandparents, relatives, and friends.

This little book, an essential companion for first-time parents and comfort for all parents, brings the reassuring voice of a wise and caring pediatrician into your home to answer every question, as it arises, even those 2 a.m. questions requiring an immediate answer.

Beverly Kilman, Ph.D
Child Psychologist
San Diego, CA

Introduction

As a young medical student, it never occurred to me to be anything but a pediatrician. I loved visiting the babies in the nurseries during my internship and residency, and time spent with children of all ages was always special. Now the babies and children I cared for during the beginning of my pediatric practice are having babies of their own. It is always a red-letter day when one of my "babies" brings her child for a visit or sends me a picture.

Parenting today is much more difficult than it was in the past. There are too many choices, new worries, and too much marketing for infants' and kids' products. Many parents get caught up in the, "keeping up with the Joneses syndrome". It is far more important for parents to keep their kids safe and spend time with them than to buy the latest in clothes, equipment, or toys.

I hope this book will be a helpful resource for parents of infants and small children. Because doctors spend less time with parents and kids these days, there are multiple questions that get unanswered. This book should provide many answers for all the questions you have, making parenting easier and more fun.

Section I

Birth to 18 Months

1. General Advice

1. As parents, you will, and must quickly, become the experts with your baby. Trust you own gut feelings and common sense. As you gain more self-confidence, you will or should realize that you are the experts with your child. Don't let anyone try to tell you differently.

> The mother of two little patients brought in a friend and her new baby for a second opinion. The baby's pediatrician had told her the infant's almost constant crying was due to colic. The baby's mother was concerned that the infant had a hard time having a bowel movement and wondered if something was wrong with the bowel. I did a rectal exam and felt a tight band of tissue just inside the rectal sphincter. By slowly putting pressure on this band, I felt it relax. The baby stopped crying and expelled a large amount of gas and stool. (These inner bands are not too common but do occur.) From that moment on, the baby became a happy, placid infant. The mother was right to trust her own instincts.

2. Anxious parents can make anxious babies. Spending time away from your baby is important, as is finding ways to relax even when you are at home. Exercise, music, yoga, taking deep breaths, and getting enough rest and good food can all help.

> One new mother found that even a 15 minute walk with someone else watching the baby made all the difference in her days.

3. It's important to establish a regular routine as soon as possible. By a routine, I mean a regular time for a nap, bedtime and the same feeding schedule. These do not have to be rigid times but approximate. This is better for your baby and for you as parents. Being constantly at your baby's "beck and call" isn't good for anyone. It creates problems that can be longstanding.

> A mother of her second baby told me how much easier it was to have already had one baby. She said that she and her husband didn't jump up the minute the new baby cried because they knew it was okay to let the infant fuss for a little.

2. Crying

Most parents quickly learn how to distinguish between their baby's different cries: a hunger cry, a hurt cry, tired cry, an angry cry, a colicky cry, and an uncomfortable cry with a soiled diaper. Wait for a few minutes when crying starts to see whether it continues and what it means. Babies need to learn and will learn to quiet themselves when they are just being fussy. *A few minutes of crying will not hurt a baby.*

No baby needs to be picked up the minute he or she starts crying. Usually babies in big families are quieter than first babies because no one has time to pick them up the minute they start crying. Letting a baby cry for five minutes is okay, unless it is a hurt cry, or the baby is crying at full volume. Most new parents can stand only a few minutes of crying. If a baby is screaming in pain, you will want to look for the cause right away.

4. Too much fussing over or stimulating a baby can cause problems. Babies need time to sleep and just "be". If they are handled too much, they get irritable and upset.

> I was waiting in an airport lounge for a flight and saw a young mother with a small baby. She and a friend constantly fussed over the baby while the infant cried and cried. I wanted to suggest to the mother that she let the baby alone, but decided she might resent the intrusion. It was a relief to have the flight called and get away from the anxious mother and unhappy baby.

5. Most babies love motion. Being rocked in a cradle or rocking chair calms a baby, as does a car ride. Walking with an infant and patting the back can be soothing. Soft music can also help.

I had a late night call from an anxious, upset father. The man said his wife was gone for the evening, and their baby wouldn't stop crying. I had just checked the baby that day, so didn't think he was ill. I gave the daddy a list of suggestions about what to do and then said, "As a last resort, you can go for a ride in the car." The father answered me very seriously, "With or without the baby?" (A parents' class might have helped this father feel more confident.)

6. When babies are dressed too warmly, they can be miserable They won't stop crying until they get a little cooler. A room that is overheated can also cause problems. Most pediatricians recommend the room temperature should be 68-72 degrees.

I was invited to a baby's christening in an old, historic church. It was an exceptionally hot day and I felt sorry for the infant dressed in the family's lovely, heirloom christening gown, slip, hat, and bootees. As the church service continued, the baby became restless and started crying loudly. I was sitting right behind the parents and leaned forward whispering, "I think Heather is very warm. Why don't you take off her hat and fan her, so she can cool down?" With some cool air, the baby stopped crying, and peace reigned once again in the church.

7. Other causes of crying include a fever, ear infection, excessive household noise, being overtired, constipation, or a wet, cold or dirty diaper. A loud TV or shouting family members can be disturbing. Sometimes, a pacifier, a drink of water or dilute apple juice will help. If a baby needs to burp after a feeding and hasn't done so, this can cause crying. Keeping a baby upright for about 20 minutes after a feeding may help. Burping can be done over the shoulder, holding the baby on your lap while supporting the back, rubbing the tummy or across your lap, and patting the back all at once.

Two young parents were desperate for a good night's sleep because their new baby cried so much. Their pediatrician couldn't find anything wrong and had no suggestions that helped. The grandmother lived close by and suggested that she take the baby overnight, so the parents could have a good night's sleep. The mother and father were delighted, and off the baby went to the grandmother's house. She thought she was in for a sleepless night, but the baby slept all night! When the parents heard this, they couldn't believe their ears. "What are we doing wrong?" they asked. The grandmother took the baby again the next night and once again the infant slept through the night.

With the grandmother's help, the parents realized that three things were different at their house. There were two dogs that barked loudly near the baby's window, the parents watched TV in the evening, and the walls were quite thin. Once the parents turned down the volume of the TV or used earphones, and the neighbors did something about their dogs, the baby had no trouble sleeping.

---

8. **True colic has a very specific pattern: Crying usually starts around 6 p.m. and is loud and ear-shattering.** The cause may be difficult to determine, but I would be sure your baby does not have a burp that needs to come up, is not hungry or over-fed, and is not allergic to milk. Sometimes, it helps for a nursing mother to stop drinking caffeine for a while. A small percentage of colic is caused by gastric reflux, or stomach juices that go back up the esophagus or feeding tube. True colic usually stops by about three months. Soft music, motion of some kind, and relaxed parents make a difference.

Gastrointestinal reflux, or GERD, seems to be in vogue now. Frequently, babies are referred to pediatric gastroenterologists or put on anti-spasmodic drugs. This may be before simple things are tried such as restricting the mother's diet if she is breast feeding, keeping the baby upright for 20 minutes after each feeding and slightly elevating the head of the baby's bed. I don't remember ever putting a baby on anti-spasmodic drugs or referring them to a pediatric gastroenterologist during the years of my practice. Usually, the simple remedies are the best.

As a young medical student, I was babysitting for a classmate and his wife. They had not warned me that Nancy had colic. When she suddenly let out a piercing cry, I was startled and not sure what to do. I tried burping Nancy, giving her a bottle, a pacifier, and walking with her, but nothing helped. Finally in desperation, I grabbed Dr. Spock's book from a nearby table and looked up crying. The book suggested a hot water bottle might help. I had seen one in the baby's room, so I filled it with warm water, wrapped a towel around it, and put it on my lap. By laying Nancy across my lap on the warm water bottle and patting her back, I finally got the crying to stop. (The parents apologized that they had forgotten to warn me about the colic.)

3. Breast and Bottle Feeding

9. Breast feeding should be special and not a chore. If it is not something a mother enjoys or the baby constantly fights the breast, it is time for bottle feeding. However, be sure you have had the best possible help to make nursing going well. If you are overtired or stressed, it will be hard to nurse. Nursing can't be forced, and it should be very enjoyable.

A good nurse or nursing consultant can teach you lots of tricks. If a baby has trouble grabbing hold of the nipple, try expressing a little milk into the baby's mouth. This usually gets the nursing started. Be sure to pull your breast away from the baby's nose and if a baby has a stuffy nose, it will be hard for the infant to nurse. You can try suctioning out mucus with a soft rubber bulb syringe. If a breast is engorged, you may need to express some milk before the baby can start to nurse. Nursing on one side for twenty minutes and then ten minutes on the other side works out the best. Start on the last side for the next nursing. Nursing should not hurt, and if it does you may have a breast infection. Using the breast as a pacifier makes you more prone to a breast infection. *Don't feel guilty if nursing doesn't work out.* Many smart, successful, and happy adults were not breast-fed.

One mother tried to breast feed but soon became exhausted. Her husband had just started a new job, and he was home very little. The couple had moved recently and had made only a few friends. In desperation, the mother called her obstetrician who suggested a wonderful, practical nurse. Once "Minnie the Angel" took over, the mother got some rest and was able to sleep through the night now and then when the nurse gave the baby a bottle. The mother's milk supply increased, and mother, father, and baby were much happier.

10. Sitting in a comfortable chair or rocking chair with a pillow under the baby's head works well for many mothers. Sometimes, a pillow is also needed on the lap. Quiet and privacy while nursing are what most nursing mothers need and want. Soft music may help. It is <u>not</u> a good idea to answer the phone while you are nursing or be talking on the phone. Nursing should be a time to relax and enjoy your baby.

11. Foods to avoid when nursing are hot, spicy foods; onions; garlic; and members of the cabbage family. Some herb teas can cause diarrhea. Allergic babies may have trouble with milk products or other allergenic foods the mother is eating or drinking.

A new mother came to see me after Thanksgiving because her baby suddenly started crying and seemed miserable. The nursing had been going very well, and the mother and baby had both been enjoying it. No abnormal physical findings were present, so I asked the mother what she had eaten at their big family Thanksgiving dinner. We decided the offending food had been rutabagas. A day or so later, the baby was fine and the mother vowed never to eat rutabagas again. (I never have!)

12. Many medicines and drugs get into breast milk so it is important to check with your doctor or doctors, if you are taking any medicines. Medicine for depression or seizures (convulsions), sleeping, and tranquilizers can be particular problems. Some antibiotics can also be a problem, so if you need to take one for an infection such as mastitis, the doctor should tell you if you can continue to breast feed or just pump your breasts.

13. Ways to increase the amount of breast milk are getting enough sleep, daily exercise, lots of fluid, and having an occasional beer. (Grace Kelly was said to have done this to help nursing), eating a good diet high in protein, being as relaxed as possible, and sitting in a comfortable chair with soft music playing. With your phone off, it is easier to relax.

14. Feedings can be spaced with the use of a pacifier, a few ounces of water, or some diluted apple juice. Full-term babies don't need to nurse more than every three to four hours, but premature babies need to eat frequently and this should be discussed with the infant's doctor. Some nursing consultants urge that a baby should be breast-fed whenever they cry. From my own experience and that of hundreds of my nursing mothers, I have found this can be exhausting. Increased fatigue usually decreases the milk supply.

> A young mother called me in tears saying she was worn out because her son wanted to nurse every hour or two. The baby was full-term, doing a lot of spitting up and had gained an excessive amount of weight. Once the mother started spacing the feedings to every three to four hours with water and diluted apple juice, mother, father, and infant son were much happier.

15. There are some dos and don'ts for bottle feeding.

- Preemies may need a special, soft nipple.
- If milk comes out too slowly, a different nipple with a larger hole needs to be used.
- Never leave a bottle in a baby's bed or prop a bottle.
- Feedings can be spaced out with a pacifier, water, or diluted apple juice.
- Babies need the closeness they get from being held for a feeding.

- Microwaving a baby's bottle is not wise. The milk will not heat uniformly and could burn a baby's mouth. Instead, you can warm milk in a pan of hot water or run hot water over it.

- Some mothers give babies a cold bottle of milk without warming it.

- You can check the temperature of the milk by putting a little on your wrist. Warm milk seems kinder to a baby's stomach.

- If a baby spits up after each feeding, make sure there isn't a burp that needs to come up. The formula may need to be changed, or the baby may need to be kept upright for twenty minutes after each feeding. These things should be tried before any medicine is given.

A new mother, who was bottle feeding her baby, complained that the infant spit up after every feeding. I watched the mother give a bottle and noticed that the little boy was gulping down the milk. I suggested two things: first, a nipple with a smaller hole should be used, and second, to keep David upright for twenty minutes after a feeding. These both seemed to help, and the mother was delighted.

4. Sleeping

16. Babies like to be in a small, snug bed, or bassinet. A crib is fine for later, but not for little ones. Even a well-padded dresser drawer can be used in an emergency. Little ones like to be bundled or swaddled in a soft blanket to sleep, unless the room is too hot. There are also some cute, zipped little suits that make it unnecessary to use a blanket, and the SIDS Foundation recommends a "Halo Sleep Sack". A warm room may keep a baby awake and cause fussiness.

One baby cried the minute she was put down in her big crib. The grandmother was visiting one day and suggested that a small, snug bassinet would help. This proved to be the answer.

17. Babies need to sleep on a firm mattress with no soft pillows or quilts. Having stuffed animals in the bed is not a good idea either. It is dangerous for an infant to sleep in a bed with the parents, and the number of infants who have suffocated while sleeping with adults has risen sharply. Suffocation can also occur in cribs that are not safe. If Venetian blinds are near a crib, an infant can get caught in the cord.

18. Infants should sleep on their backs, not the side or face, as parents were told in the past. It has been determined that there is an increased incidence of SIDS or sudden infant death, when babies sleep on the side or face. *The use of a pacifier seems to help decrease the number of SIDS deaths, as does a smoke-free environment.*

19. **When a baby is put into a crib, it is important to check that the crib slats are no more than 2-3/8 inches apart.** Babies have caught their necks in cribs with wider slats. Old cribs that are painted with lead paint should not be used. The mattress should fit firmly in the crib and the crib should not have cutouts at either end because babies have been caught in these.

20. **A music box by the bed, a white noise machine, or a well secured mobile** overhead may help the baby settle down and go to sleep. Signs of tiredness can be rubbing the eyes, cranky cries, and yawning. If a baby is restless, check for a burp, a soiled or wet diaper. Be sure too that the little one is not hungry. A pacifier can be a life saver, as can a rocking chair. Be sure there is not a nearby loud, blaring TV, radio, or loud conversations. Most babies nap for about two hours at a time and parents should soon see a pattern showing the length of time a baby will sleep. If the infant sleeps unusually long, this could be a signal that there is a fever or an illness is brewing.

5. Bathing

21. A warm bath can be very soothing for a baby. Be sure your baby is not hungry and fussy, then bath time can be miserable for everyone. Check the water temperature carefully before the bath, and be sure that the water heater is set at 120 degrees Fahrenheit or lower. Sponge baths are best until the cord and circumcision are healed. A towel in the bottom of a tub can prevent slipping. Some mothers like to give their baby an evening bath, so fathers may be able to take over.

22. Expensive soaps, shampoos, and powders are not necessary. Cornstarch is a good powder, and baby oils and lotions are usually not needed. Be careful about keeping powder away from the baby's face.

> I was standing in line behind a frazzled-looking woman in a grocery store check-out line. Her basket was filled with diapers, baby lotion, oil, shampoo, and soap for which the woman paid with food stamps. I wished she had used the food stamps to buy some good food for herself and wanted to tell her that simple soaps and cornstarch were the best. The more things you put on a baby's skin, the greater chance for an allergic reaction.

23. Babies usually enjoy a daily bath. Even if they are gently cleaned after being wet or having a bowel movement, they still can get pretty grubby. Babies love being clean and dry after a bath. *Never, ever, leave a baby alone in a bath*, even for a few seconds; just let the telephone or doorbell ring. Also, don't leave an infant alone on a changing table, but have everything you need for a bath within easy reach. Because of the increased temperature of the water in a Jacuzzi, babies should <u>never </u>be taken into one.

24. Fingernails need to be kept short. One person can hold the baby, while another cuts the nails. If the nails are hard to cut, little mitts can be used, so your baby can't scratch his or her face. Some parents prefer to cut their child's nails when the baby is asleep. Other parents like to use a soft emery board to file the nails.

6. Babies with Special Needs

25. It takes special parents to successfully raise babies born with disabilities or those who develop problems within the first few months. Finding a physician who is willing, has the knowledge, and takes the time to find and coordinate the best care will make all the difference in the world. By talking with other parents, social workers, and nurses, it should be possible to find this physician. A general pediatrician who will work in conjunction with specialists may be the one you want.

26. If the baby has a so-called "birth defect", it is important that the state agency for these babies be notified within the first few days after birth, if you will need financial assistance. Each state has an agency to help with the care of children who have disabilities. (See Appendix)

> One family had a baby born with spina bifida. They had limited financial resources, and the nursery staff didn't tell them they needed to immediately call the state agency that is responsible for children with disabilities. The hospital bill, for which they were responsible, exceeded $100,000. They were devastated by the baby's disability and didn't know what to do. Fortunately, an excellent social worker worked with them to resolve the financial problem.

27. If your baby is a preemie or needs to stay in the intensive care nursery unit for a period of time, it is most important that mothers, in particular, don't "live" at the hospital, but do at least some of their daily tasks or work. It is easy to become "burned out" if you spend all your days and some nights at the hospital. The intensive care nurses and doctors usually do a wonderful job of caring for babies, and you do not want to interfere if you are comfortable with the care your baby is receiving. Relatives and friends can offer help and relieve a parent, so don't be afraid to ask. Many people will be delighted to assist with shopping and even cooking for a while. It is also important if other children are in the family that they are not neglected. It is particularly hard for siblings when a new baby is born with a disability. If all the parents' attention is focused on the baby, siblings will begin to feel lonely, rejected, and unloved. Lifetime patterns begin early, so it is extremely important that the siblings receive the attention they deserve. A sibling group may be the answer for kids with a special needs brother or sister. Grandparents, who live nearby, may also offer much needed help.

28. Support groups exist for almost every type of disability. These can provide tremendous support, and most groups put out newsletters with valuable information. The National Organization for Rare Diseases will provide you with a wealth of information and can be contacted at: 1-800-999-NORD or on their website, **www.rarediseases.org**. Other parents with a special needs baby or child usually have a wealth of information they are glad to share. They can also offer support. Many organizations for special disabilities have group meetings and often picnics or holiday parties. Meeting another child with a similar disability can make a great different to a child.

29. Every parent who has an infant born with a disability or one who develops a problem within the first few months needs to take time to grieve. Unless grieving is done, pain and anger will come out in forms of depression, medical issues, or emotional problems at some time in the future. Parent, mothers' and fathers' groups of special needs children usually offer a great deal of support and information. Individual counseling may also be needed. Grieving goes through different stages: shock, denial, fear, anger, guilt, and sometimes rejection. Grief affects people in different ways; some numb their pain and others try to bury it. This doesn't work because the pain will come out eventually in a destructive way or medical problem. Allowing yourself to grieve for a few minutes each day will help lessen the pain. To do this, find a quiet place where you can cry, throw, or pound something. It is important to take extra care of yourself while you are grieving.

Section II

Infants and Children

7. Clothing

30. Flameproof clothing should always be used. (Some European clothing is not flameproof.) There should be a tag on each piece of clothing that tells if it is flameproof. Halloween costumes always need to be checked to be sure they are flame-resistant. Costumes offer a particular problem because of lighted candles and other Halloween decorations. Clothing with tight drawstrings that go around the neck should never be used because drawstrings can cause choking. Tight necklaces should also be avoided because of a possibility of choking.

31. Babies and children don't like to be dressed too warmly. If babies are too hot, then they can become very fussy. Cotton, not nylon or wool clothing, is the best kind to have next to a child's skin. Children-Next-to-New shops can save considerable money, and often you can recycle clothing that has had little to no wear. What a baby has on should mimic the parents' clothing, unless you get unusually hot or cold. If you dress warmly, your baby needs to be warmly dressed also, but if it is hot, then your baby should not be bundled in layers of clothing.

> I was walking on a beach one hot day and saw a father with a crying little one in his arms. He was very upset and said, "I can't get her to stop crying." The baby was dressed in several layers, was red in the face, and looked miserable. I suggested she would be happier without so many clothes and that a sunsuit and hat were all she needed. The father thanked me, took off several layers of the baby's clothing, and the baby stopped crying.

32. Hats are important for cold weather and hot weather. Babies should be protected from the sun on hot days with hats and from the cold on wintery days, especially if they have a respiratory infection or have been ill. (I've seen many parents with hats on in cold and hot weather and yet their babies didn't have hats on. This always puzzles me.) Even tiny babies are often outside in a parent's arms on very hot summer days with nothing on their heads.

33. Shoes are not needed until babies start pulling up or walking. However, some kind of protection for the feet is needed, particularly in cold weather. When it is time to buy shoes, check to be sure there is a thumb nails room in front of the big toe. Children grow so quickly that you don't want to buy shoes that are too small.

I was walking on a hot sidewalk in the city when I saw a two-year-old and her mother. The little girl was dressed in a pink sundress and was barefoot. The sidewalk was dirty, and I worried that the child was going to step on a sharp object. The mother had on shoes and seemed unaware of the possible dangers on the sidewalk.

8. Traveling

34. Traveling with infants or children can be difficult, unless careful plans have been made. People can be quite intrusive, sometimes strangers will even try to kiss your baby. As a parent, you may have to be quite standoffish to keep people away. You can say, *"I'm sorry, but I would ask that you not get so close to my baby."* It is difficult to travel alone with an infant or small child, but you have to be very careful about a person who offers help. They may be kind, but they may not know how to handle a baby or child. I would ask a flight attendant to help you on the flight or on one flight, I asked the co-pilot to hold the baby. He was walking through the main cabin, and I was desperate to use the restroom. The flight attendants were busy serving drinks.

> I was flying across country with a three-week-old baby and couldn't believe how many strangers, even those with colds, tried to hug or kiss Jennifer. I had to keep her covered, as much as possible, and act quite unfriendly, though this was difficult for me.

35. It is important to carry twice as many supplies as you think you will need, if you are flying, going by bus or train, or driving. Babies and little children can go through lots of diapers and clothing in a very short time. A first-aid kit, thermometer, and flashlight are also important to carry. (I always carry a bag that contains supplies and snacks, drinks, and surprises for older children.) Now, you can't carry fluids on airplanes, but since the regulations keep changing, you need to call or check an airline's website, if you are going to fly with an infant or child.

A young mother brought her baby in for a check-up before she made a long car trip to meet her military husband. I asked when she was leaving and she said, "As soon as you finish checking Mary". When I asked what supplies she was taking, her answer was "I plan to pick up things along the way. I've been too busy and too tired to go shopping." We put together a kit with bottles of formula, diapers, and other things and sent the mother and baby on their way. I asked the young mother to call when she arrived to let us know she had arrived safely. I was relieved to get her call.

36. Infants and children need to continuously suck on a bottle or pacifier when an airplane is taking off or landing. If a little one has a cold, this is even more important. Otherwise, a painful ear can result from a pressure build-up, and you will have a crying, miserable baby. I would check with your baby's doctor before leaving on a trip to see if Tylenol or other medication should be given. However, I would never give an infant or child medication that had not been given previously. One mother did this and had a screaming, irritable child the whole flight.

I was flying to a medical meeting in England, when soon after the airplane took off, a struggling, screaming boy was brought to the front of the plane. His mother was with him and seemed frantic. The youth screamed and thrashed around for the entire flight. We finally landed in London and an ambulance met the airplane. I wished the mother had talked with a physician before leaving her home and tried some medication that could have been used on the trip. I felt sad for the boy, his mother, and all the passengers.

37. If you are staying in a hotel or motel, it is important to check the crib in which the baby or little child will sleep. If you are driving and can carry your own bed that is better. You can also purchase a portable crib that folds flat and is easy to carry. The crib slats on any crib should be no more than 2-3/8 inches apart because babies can stick their heads between the slats and get caught. The mattress should be firm and soft pillows or quilts must not be in the bed. Cribs with cutouts at the foot or head of the bed are unsafe, as are loose or missing screws. Some babies don't sleep well in an unfamiliar bed. One couple books a suite room, so they can talk or watch TV and the baby can sleep in another room. They say this is often not much more expensive. Always check that a room has functioning smoke and carbon monoxide detectors, and the windows have guards or don't open more than a few inches.

Two children, ages two and four, traveled with their parents to an aunt's wedding in the east. The wedding was being held in an elegant hotel and the family was given a very nice room on the eighth floor. Fortunately, the mother and father knew to check the room for problems as soon as they entered. It was good they did because the windows opened about two feet, and there were no guards! Either one of the active children could have climbed through the open windows and handed on the hard pavement eight stories below. For several months after the wedding, one of the grandmothers sent letters and made phone calls trying to get the large hotel chain to put guards on all their windows. Finally, the CEO answered saying that it had been done.

---

9. Equipment

....

38. Most parents think they have to have the latest in baby beds, strollers, and other equipment. Often beds, bassinets, playpens, and other things can be borrowed, but be sure that no lead-containing paint has been used on beds, playpens, or bassinets. Some community or parents' groups have equipment exchanges, and because babies and little children grow so quickly this is a way to save money. An approved car seat is a must, so an old one may not be the best.

39. The approved car seat for infants is from birth to twenty pounds, or under one year of age is a rear-facing infant restraint. No infant's car seat should ever be put in front of an air bag. A good resource for vehicle safety information is: **National Highway Traffic Safety Administration** at: **1-800-424-9393** or their website at **www.nhtsa.gov.** After 20 pounds, a different car seat can be used. A pamphlet can be obtained from your child's doctor or from the Auto Safety 800 number about which car seat to use. If you have trouble installing a car seat, check with your local fire or police departments to see if they can help. Some hospitals offer help, and highway patrol officers may also offer assistance.

40. The expensive strollers that have a place on top for a coffee cup are not only expensive but also worrisome. Having hot coffee on top of an infant or child's head and face is not safe. Carrying a cup of hot coffee, while pushing a baby or child in a stroller is also risky.

41. Playpens are extremely important for infants and toddlers once they are in the crawling stage. This way a parent or child-care person can safely do a chore without worrying about the baby. Gates at stairs and some doors may also be necessary. If a mesh playpen is used as a little one gets older, make sure there are no holes in the mesh because small children have been caught in these. For some reason these days, a myth has been perpetuated that playpens retard development. **This is absolutely wrong.** My patients, my own children and grandchildren have never shown any developmental delay because playpens were used. Playpens could also have saved their lives from a bad accident, electrical burn, or other dangerous situation.

I made a house call one day for an ill child who had reached the crawling stage. The small house had a basement with stairs leading down from the dining area. For some reason, the mother was resistant to the idea of a playpen, even though the grandparents had urged her to buy one. When the father walked me to my car, I told him it was not safe to let the baby crawl around on the floor, particularly if the door to the basement was left open. No parent can watch a baby every minute; the telephone or doorbell may ring, or the trash may need to be taken outside. The father promised he would buy a playpen that afternoon, and I was relieved.

10. Emergencies

42. All parents and babysitters should know what to do in an emergency.
911 can be called, but there are things that should be done before an ambulance or fire truck arrives. CPR courses are given by the American Red Cross and by some hospitals. There are also CPR videos that can be purchased online by typing in CPR training. If an infant or child is choking, stops breathing, or has a convulsion or seizure, the most important thing is to be sure there is a clear airway. Some parents use a monitor in their child's room to be sure they can always hear normal breathing.

Small objects such as pins, buttons, coins, or beads should never be where a baby can grab and put them in the mouth. Peanuts can be particularly lethal if a baby or little child puts one in his or her mouth. Hard candies, chunks of cheese, popcorn, small magnets, marshmallows, sunflower seeds, fish and chicken with bones, and raw vegetables can all cause choking.

I was on an airplane one day when there was a call for a physician. A baby, who was a crawler, had been allowed down on the floor of the plane and put a peanut in her mouth. She was choking and turning blue. Fortunately, I was able to dislodge the peanut and get the child breathing again. (I hoped the mother would have second thoughts before letting her baby crawl around another time on an airplane floor.)

43. True emergencies include:

- Convulsions or seizures

- Loss of consciousness

- Choking or difficulty breathing

- Excessive sleeping or listlessness

- Eye injury

- Severe, uncontrolled bleeding

- Fracture of a bone

- High fever

- Fall from a height

- Prolonged vomiting or diarrhea

- Head injury

- Severe burn

- Severe allergic reaction

- Rash (petechiae) that spreads quickly in an ill baby or child

- Stiffness of the neck

- Severe croup

- Electric shock

- A child who is out of control

- Near drowning

- Severe abdominal pain

- Gun-shot wound (**Even small children may be exposed to guns.**)

It is important to know that not all ERs have the necessary equipment to care for childhood emergencies. If you move to a new town or have a new doctor, I would check with him or her to see if the hospital the doctor uses has the necessary pediatric equipment. If not, it is wise to know where your child should be taken if there is an emergency that requires special pediatric equipment.

Even little children can be taught about what to do in an emergency.

> When my son was about three, he was playing in our back yard with some neighborhood children. I was near a window, so I could watch the children playing. Suddenly, Geoffrey burst into the house and said "Mommy, the children are all going to have their stomachs pumped out." I ran into the yard to see a little boy passing out pills from an old purse. Geoffrey had heard me talk about pumping out a child's stomach and knew something was wrong.

44. No baby or small child should be allowed to have a rectal temperature over 101-102 degrees without the parent talking to the baby's <u>doctor</u> or having the child seen. Babies and little children can become ill very quickly, and meningitis does occur even in little ones. Every parent should know how to take a rectal temperature and have a rectal thermometer on hand. (Rectal temperatures are easy to take and are the most accurate. Your baby's doctor or nurse can show you how to take a rectal temperature.) *A baby or child <u>must</u> always be seen before a prescription for an antibiotic is called into a pharmacy from a doctor's office.* Any fever should be treated with cooling measures and Tylenol, as prescribed by your doctor. ER doctors often do not have the training to see a child with a fever.

45. Post the emergency numbers of your local poison center, the doctor, and the closest hospital by your house phone or add in your cell phone. The **National Poison Center** can be reached at: **1-800-222-1222.** Syrup of Ipecac, which was used in the past to induce vomiting, is no longer recommended. Instead, going immediately to the nearest emergency room is advised, so the poisonous substance can be removed by either a tube inserted into the stomach or by an absorbent substance. It is wise to take along the bottle, plant or whatever poisonous substance that was ingested. A call should always be made before heading to the ER to the baby's doctor so he or she can understand the situation. The doctor may want to meet you at the emergency room.

11. Medical Concerns & Tips

....

46. All babies need to be checked frequently by a pediatrician or family doctor within their first few months. Many problems are correctable if they are identified early. Children can be checked less frequently but should still be seen every two to three months when they are small or if they are having problems.

Jared, a five-month-old baby, was brought in by his parents for a check-up because they were concerned he didn't seem to be developing normally. The baby had not been seen by a doctor since his birth and had been delivered by a midwife. I was greatly concerned when I examined Jared. He was listless, pale, had dry skin, and was also constipated, according to his parents. I suspected the thyroid gland was not functioning properly and this had resulted in low thyroid production (hypothyroidism). The baby also appeared to be anemic. Lab tests proved both to be true.

Once thyroid medication and iron were started, Jared gradually began to develop normally and lose all signs of hypothyroidism and anemia. If the parents had waited to see a doctor much longer, their son could have been permanently damaged intellectually.

47. It is important for a baby or little child to be seen by a baby doctor if there is:

- Poor weight gain or loss
- Poor suck in an infant
- Decreased appetite

- Little movement or listlessness

- Breathing problems

- A yellow color to the skin or eyes

- Oozing or infection around the navel

- Pus oozing from the eyes

- High-pitched or non-stop crying

- No initial bowel movement or wet diapers

- <u>Your instincts say something is wrong</u>

- Diarrhea

- Elevated temperature

48. Immunizations are important to give according to the schedule your pediatrician gives you. *<u>No connection has been established between autism and immunizations.</u>* Mumps, whooping cough and other childhood diseases are being seen again and can cause severe disability or deaths if infants and children are not protected. (See immunization chart in Appendix.) Tuberculin skin tests are important every one to two years. In states such as California, where there is an increased incidence of tuberculosis, yearly skin tests are wise. If a child is found to have tuberculosis within the first year and it is not detected for two years, a delay in treatment could be serious. (You may have to insist your child receives a TB skin test. Some doctors are lax in giving these.)

49. Medical Tips:

- **If your baby has an obstructed tear duct,** try massage and warm compresses for several days before allowing the duct to be surgically opened. Gentle massage for a few days at the inner corner of the eye will often open an obstructed tear duct.

- **Boy babies can develop a large collection of a cheesy substance called smega** under their foreskin. By gently pulling back or retracting the foreskin, if this is possible, smega can be removed. Baby girls also may have a cheesy material between the folds of the labia. Sometimes, in the early days they can have a little vaginal discharge and even a little vaginal bleeding.

I was asked to consult about a baby boy in a hospital intensive care unit, and as I was doing an examination, I noticed a large swelling around the tip of the baby's penis. I assumed it was an accumulation of smega and asked the nurse to bring me some gauze squares. By gently pulling back the baby's foreskin, I removed the smega. Two pediatric residents were watching me and seemed horrified by what I had done. When I asked them why they were upset, one said "Dr. A, the head of the ICU, said the swelling around the penis was due to a tumor." I tried to keep from laughing and explained what smega was and that it was not a tumor! (I was never Dr. A's favorite consultant after that.)

- **New babies may have a milky discharge from the nipples.** The breasts can also be enlarged or engorged in both boy and girl babies. This usually lasts just a short while.

- **An infant or child with a high, unexplained fever should <u>always</u> have a urine specimen checked.** (There are special infant and small child urine collection bags.) Meningitis can also occur in babies and little children and if there is any suspicion of this, a spinal tap needs to be done. This is not a difficult procedure in an infant or child.

- **Q-Tips should never be used in a baby or child's ear.** They can cause damage and push wax down into the ear canal. The external ear can be gently cleaned with a washcloth. A physician can clean an ear canal under direct vision by looking through an otoscope and using an instrument called an ear curet.

- **Bowing of the legs is normal in babies and little children,** but the legs should begin to straighten out once a child starts walking. A difference is leg lengths is important to notice in babies, particularly in girls, because this could be due to a congenital dislocation of the hip. If this is identified early, the hip can be treated and corrected.

- **Babies and little children may develop flatness of the head** because of sleeping on their back. Once they start moving around and turning over, this should disappear. There are some congenital abnormalities of the head that do need treatment. Special helmets have been devised for some of the abnormalities and once in a while surgery will be needed, but this is rare. Helmets have now proved to not make a difference in the shape of a baby's head.

- **Most hemangiomas, which are red and raised small, soft collections of blood vessels get smaller or will disappear as a child grows older.** A pediatric dermatologist always needs to be consulted before a physician does anything to one of these. Otherwise severe scarring may result. Most large port wine stains on the face can be treated with a laser when a child is older. You might want to get one or two opinions about the time to do this.

- **Any baby who is not making sounds by three months of age** should have a hearing exam by a qualified hearing professional. Older children with frequent ear infections and delayed speech should also have their hearing checked in a pediatric hearing center. Thirty-eight states mandate that the newborns' hearing must be checked before they leave the hospital. However, there can always be an error in the testing, so if a baby is not making sounds by three months, a repeat testing should be done in a pediatric hearing center, not a doctor's office.

- **Babies who are teething usually don't have elevated temperatures.** They can be fussy and miserable, but should always be checked for an ear infection or other cause. Cold teething rings, rubbing the gums with a clean finger, and teething biscuits all help.

- **An infant or child can have an ear infection without having an elevated temperature.** The child may just be a little fussy or an older child may pull at the ear. A child may also keep his head turned to the side of the infected ear. If a baby or child has a cough or cold, be sure your doctor checks the ears. Ears are often infected along with a respiratory infection.

- **If a baby boy does not have a good urinary stream** or the opening at the tip of the penis seems to be off-center, the doctor needs to be alerted.

- **Baby boys may have their scrotums filled with fluid.** This is called a hydrocele and is quite common at birth. The fluid usually absorbs by six months.

- **Diaper rash** can usually be cleared by keeping the diaper area as clean as possible and using Zinc oxide ointment or Eucerin's aquafor.

- **Milia** is the term for tiny white spots that occur around the nose in newborns. Spots should disappear in a few days or weeks and need no treatment.

- **Thrush** is a fungus infection in the mouth caused by monilia. It can be treated with special medicine from your doctor. Some diaper rashes are also caused by monilia and have a different appearance from the usual diaper rash. This rash is usually red and raised.

12. Time for Mothers

50. It is important not to lose your individuality after having a baby. You are still a person with your own personality and interests and should not make the baby your whole life. If you do, both you and your child will eventually pay a price for this; medical problems, anger, or depression can result. If you find yourself becoming depressed or angry, let your doctor know. Some medication or counseling could be the answer.

An older, first-time mother sat tensely holding her baby in her lap. She had been a very successful professional and was having difficulty staying home with the baby. "I've been in charge of a major division at work," the mother said, "but this little 8 lbs. boy is controlling my life. We have a nanny, but she makes me feel inadequate. I'm losing my confidence, and I'm afraid our marriage will suffer. What am I doing wrong?"

51. Connect with friends and other mothers as often as possible. Local parks, chat rooms, book groups, and mothers' groups are all ways to stay in touch with others. For some mothers, spending time alone reading in a library can help. Interacting with others in a coffee shop, the cleaners, grocery store, or department stores can also make every day seem normal again and pass by more quickly. Remember that not all mothers love staying at home with a new baby. Even though a mother loves her infant doesn't mean she enjoys changing diapers, feeding her baby, and everything else that goes along with having a small child.

52. Plan some daily time for yourself right from the beginning. A friend, relative, neighbor, hired babysitter, or your partner could watch the baby for awhile. If a father works at home or can help on the weekend, then he can become more involved with an infant. It is hard for a mother to be in the house if a father is taking over because it is too easy to interfere and not let the father take charge. Fathers need to feel comfortable taking full charge of a child. Sometimes, they are more relaxed than mothers, who have been at a baby's beck and call. Exercise, time alone in a coffee shop or park can all help keep your life in balance. Fifteen minutes a day for you is important, just as is one to two hours a week. A hot bath or massage can relieve stress, as can having some fun. Don't wait too long to start taking care of yourself.

53. It is important to plan a weekly date with your husband or partner. Fathers often feel left out, if a mother is breast-feeding or starts devoting herself entirely to the baby. When you spend time with your mate, don't talk about your baby. With an older child, it is still important to have weekly time together. A babysitter is an important part of your support system and mini-vacations are needed. Many mothers wait until the child is walking to have a babysitter. _This is much too late._ Infants and children will be fine with a babysitter from any age, as long as you have carefully checked the sitter's recommendations and credentials.

I had one mother who loved breast feeding and didn't want to give her 2-year-old any bottles. Her husband wanted them to take a weekend trip to San Francisco, but the woman didn't want to leave her child, even though they had a nanny and a grandmother close by. I felt the couple needed some time alone and the trip would be important. I was a young, divorced woman and said, "Either you go with him or I will!" The mother was not sure if I meant it, which I didn't, but I worried her enough that she agreed to go and the couple had a great time.

13. Time for Fathers

....

54. Treat your self to something special now and then. Don't put all of your energy into work and your baby or child. If you do, you may start resenting having so little time to yourself. If you take care of yourself before taking care of your family, then you can do a better job for everyone.

> A young father called me in despair one evening. "My wife has gone back to work", he said, "and I'm the chief caretaker. We have a cleaning woman and eat simply, so those are not the problem. It's the baby, who never seems happy. I must be doing something wrong. I greatly fear for my own survival and our other two kids are suffering. I'm also worried about our marriage." My diagnosis after checking Ryan was that there was nothing physically wrong, but he had poor weight gain and was irritable. I suspected a milk allergy. Once the cow's milk formula was stopped, the baby became placid and gained weight.

55. Try to get some daily exercise or, if possible, several times a week. This will make the stress of taking care of a baby or child much easier. Also, plan some weekly time to do just what you want. Having time with a buddy or friends to have some fun can be a great stress reliever.

56. Try to plan some weekly fun time with your wife or partner. Don't discuss the baby or children! This doesn't have to involve a big expenditure of money. Most towns and cities offer free museum nights, art gallery openings, and other events that take little or no money. Going on a picnic can be great fun.

57. Join a fathers' group if you are feeling left out or overwhelmed by your new baby or kids. If you prefer talking to one person rather than being involved in a huge group, discuss troublesome issues with a sympathetic friend or find a good counselor. There are also fathers' online chat groups. Fathers' classes can be very helpful, and many hospitals give them. All fathers need to be reminded how important they are to their children. Nothing can replace a father's love.

58. If your wife shows signs of post-partum depression, or depression later on, please get immediate professional help for her. Your internist or the obstetrician should be able to recommend someone good. The signs of post-partum depression are: frequent crying, sleeping a lot, irritability, inability to sleep, frequent outbursts of anger and on-going unhappiness, sadness and a fear of hurting the new baby. Hiring some household help for her will also make a difference. Little babies can take over a mother's life and make it difficult to accomplish everything she may want to do. Getting her out of the house and away from the baby can also be very helpful. Going for a walk, getting a cup of tea or coffee or an afternoon treat can make the world look a lot rosier.

14. Multiple Births

59. Twins and triplets can be lots of fun but extremely stressful without plenty of help. Grandparents, neighborhood teenagers, college students, and paid helpers make all the difference in the world. If you try to be super-parents and get along without any help, something is bound to happen. It is better to pay for help than to not have any if that is the only way to have daily help. If you can decrease your stress, fatigue, and anxiety, the short and long-term dividends will be many. There may be mothers who will gladly trade babysitting time, which would save considerable money. Medical students can also be a resource. Just having a teenager help after school can make a difference and not cost that much.

Grandparents and other relatives can be of tremendous help. One family had one child, then triplet girls, and finally twin boys. The babies arrived with little space in between them, and the parents were exhausted. They had six children under age 4 with most of them in diapers. A grandmother moved in and stayed for several years.

60. Twin and triplet clubs can offer much support and guidance. Some of these groups also have equipment exchanges and newsletters. It is not necessary to have everything brand new. The only cautions are to watch out for old cribs and playpens that were painted with lead paint or crib slats that are more than 2 3/8 inches apart. Standard, approved car seats are a must.

61. Parents of older multiple birth children or grandparents can often provide great suggestions and even help. Don't be shy about asking questions. Some general tips about multiple-birth children are:

- Treat each child as a distinct personality

- Try not to dress the children alike

- If one baby or child has a disability, be sure the other children get equal time and attention

- Ask for and accept help

- Try to simplify your life as much as possible

- Let unimportant things slide

- Try to find playmates for the children, when they are old enough to enjoy them

62. Books about multiple birth babies, websites, and chat rooms can be informative and offer wise advice. Your own common sense is still the most important resource you have as parents. (See Appendix)

15. Child Care

63. All parents need to find a reliable babysitter as soon as possible. If you wait too long to have a sitter, it will get harder and harder and then may be impossible. Some mothers never want to have a babysitter, which puts their marriages in jeopardy. A babysitter may be a relative, friend, or someone hired through an agency. Even if the babysitter is a relative, you need to tell him or her how you want things done. Child care has changed since the days when grandparents raised their children, so you want to be sure older babysitters are up-to-date on childcare practices. All babysitters must know how to contact you, how the baby or child should be fed, clothed, and put in bed. They also should know basic first-aid and CPR and be able to communicate with a doctor or others.

64. If you hire someone who is not a friend, neighbor, or relative, be very sure he or she is reliable. Find out, too, if they are smokers, have medical problems, or a police record. Usually, it is possible for individuals to obtain a chest X-ray, to rule out tuberculosis, at your the local health department and fingerprinting can be done at the police department. These may seem like extreme measures, but you may have cause to be very glad both of these were done. A medical report from the individual's doctor would be another important thing to have. If financially possible, I would contact an agency, such as Nanny Care. They have a national presence and all of their nannies are thoroughly checked out. Their website is: **www.nannycare.com**. A website suggested by a former patient is **www.sittercity.com**.

Checking references is important, but remember that an individual can forge written references. I would advise giving a new childcare person a one-to-two-week trial period. If things go well, the individual could then be offered a permanent job. Some parents like to have a childcare person sign a contract. This document states exactly what is expected, the hours of work, wages, and what will and will not be tolerated: frequent personal telephone calls, visitors, smoking and similar things.

A professional mother had to go back to work and hired a childcare woman through an agency. She carefully checked the woman's references and all seemed well. For extra assurance, she asked her upstairs neighbor to check on how things were going and to call if there seemed to be any problem. The afternoon of the first day, the kind neighbor called and said, "I think you need to come home right away. The babysitter seems groggy and toothpicks and butter are all over the kitchen floor. The baby is in his crib and is OK." The mother rushed home and realized the woman needed to see a physician because she appeared to have had a convulsion or seizure. The sitter refused to be taken to a doctor and instead wanted to go to a friend's house.

Later, the mother found out that the woman did not believe in doctors and her references had been from people with her same religious beliefs. She could not believe the phone call she received a few days later from the woman asking to come back to work! No matter how carefully references are checked, there can be problems. Also, references can be forged.

65. Many resources are available to find baby sitters: such as college employment services, childcare agencies, au pair agencies, parent newsletters, friends, relatives, parent groups, senior centers and your pediatrician or family doctor. Often, you can trade childcare with another parent. Sometimes, you can share a nanny or childcare person with another mother. If your baby has special needs, respite care can often be obtained from the state program responsible for children with special needs. (See Appendix) Some insurance companies will pay for respite help and registered nurses can be paid for if this is the level of care needed. There is a difference between au pairs, childcare individuals, and sitters. Au pairs are usually from outside the U.S. and brought in by a family for a specified period of time. If an au pair is hired through an agency, you will want to make sure that the agency is well-known and reliable. A lot can fall through the cracks.

Important Information for Sitters:

All sitters need to have a list of numbers to call if there is a problem. All numbers should be posted by the principal phone or on the refrigerator. Leaving your cell phone or work number is most important, but if for some reason you are not available, several other numbers should be provided. These are:

- Your baby or child's doctor
- The nearest hospital
- Neighbors who would be at home
- Relatives who live close by
- A plumber and handyman
- The police and fire departments
- The local and national poison centers

Other important information for sitters includes:

- A list of any food or other allergies.
- The baby's or child's general routine.
- Location of fire extinguishers.
- Location of first aid kit.
- Instructions about heaters, furnaces, air conditioners or appliances that may need to be used.
- Location of the nearest grocery store.
- Instructions about any pets.

16. Siblings

66. When a new baby is brought home, siblings may be delighted or can be consumed with jealously. Jealousy is very important to prevent because otherwise a sibling might try to physically harm a baby. If there are siblings, a good way to prevent troubles is to have the new baby send little gifts home for them from the hospital. Once the baby arrives home, involving the siblings in the care will make them feel important and needed. Giving each sibling one-to-one time is very important. Every child needs to feel loved and treasured, and a new baby in the house can be upsetting. Time spent with a parent can be as simple as reading a story together, going for ice cream or a walk. One mother takes one child at a time on flower walks, and this way spends individual time with that child.

67. If a baby is a preemie or has a birth defect and has to be in the intensive care nursery for a period of time, the siblings may feel lonely and lost if the parents don't spend much time with them. Some parents, particularly mothers, almost live in the nursery when they have with a premature or special needs baby. This can wreak havoc at home both with other children and with their mate. Friends and family members can help relieve a parent. Remember, too, that hovering over the infant may make it difficult for the nurses and physicians to give the best care. Usually, the personnel in intensive care nurseries are very dedicated and excellent.

68. A latch high up on the baby's door may be needed both with siblings who love the new baby and those that don't. Siblings often sneak into a baby's room to hug a baby or to cause harm. A latch high up on a door is a good preventive measure for either situation, because no adult can constantly be on guard. Hooks can also prevent a pet from getting into a baby's room and causing harm. Cat-scratch fever does happen and can cause illness in an infant or child.

17. Finding the Best Doctors

69. **If you are looking for a doctor for your baby or child, ask your doctors, other parents, friends, and neighbors for suggestions.** It is not wise to take a name from the Yellow Pages or call your local medical society. The staff cannot make recommendations, but just give names, addresses, and telephone numbers. Be sure doctors don't just give the names of their neighbors or good friends. These may not be the ones you want. The list of the *Best Doctors* in a city is usually compiled by other doctors who they may know from a health or golf club, but not by how they practice medicine. These doctors may not be the ones you want for your child. You can check out most doctors on the Internet and also on your state Medical Board's website.

70. **Once you have done your research, try to make an appointment** with the doctor or doctors you have chosen. Some doctors won't talk to you without charging for the visit; others will. Once you find a doctor you like, be sure the staff are pleasant, and the office is clean and convenient for you to reach. I would ask several questions to be sure the doctor is right for your child.

- Does the doctor see all of his/her patients, or have a nurse practitioner or physician's assistant see some of them?

- Is the doctor board-certified or board-qualified in pediatrics or family medicine? Where did he or she have medical training?

- Does the doctor meet you in a hospital emergency room if this is needed?

- Does the doctor see children before prescribing antibiotics?

- At which hospital or hospitals does the doctor have staff privileges?

- With which doctors does he or she trade calls and how often is the doctor on-call nights and weekends?

- Does your insurance or HMO cover the doctor's services?

- Will the doctor call you with results of tests or other reports or have someone in the office call?

- Can you speak to the doctor if you need to or does a nurse or office person always take and return calls?

A young mother had just flown across country with her three-month-old little girl. The father had left earlier and found the family a house. He was starting a new job, so the mother was left with a tired baby who wouldn't stopped crying. She had been given the name of a pediatrician and called because she was desperate for help.

The phone call was referred to the doctor's nurse who said "The doctor is too busy to see your baby, and he wouldn't tell you anything that I can't tell you!" Fortunately, after a call to the pediatrician she had had as a child, the doctor did immediately see the mother and baby. The young mother later said, "I was just too worn out to fight with the nurse even though I was desperate for help." She couldn't have been more grateful to her mother and the pediatrician, who both had helped.

---

71. If you are comfortable with the doctor but want to feel completely at ease, you can check your state's medical board website. This will show if any malpractice lawsuits have been filed against him or her. Remember, however some excellent doctors settle lawsuits to save the time and money needed to contest them.

18. Finding a Different Doctor

72. If a doctor does not relate to you or your children, seems irritable, rushed, or spends little time with you, then it is time to look for a different doctor. The doctor you want should sit down, answer your questions, and make you feel comfortable with his or her examination and treatment of your children. If your questions are not answered or the doctor answers repeated phone calls or does not do a complete history and physical examination, when that is what you expect, it is time to change doctors.

73. If you need to change doctors, do lots of research and once you are satisfied you have found a good one, send or fax a written request to the doctor you have had with a request that your child's records be sent to the new doctor. It is wise to follow-up in one to two weeks to be sure this has been done. If your child has had X-rays or lab work, it is important that the new doctor see these. Copies can be made of X-rays, usually at a small charge, and you can request copies of any lab work that is done. It is a good idea to keep a separate medical file for each child. Also, keep a record of all immunizations that have been given and be sure your child receives the necessary immunizations. (See Appendix) Some doctors are not good about being sure immunizations are up-to-date. You should expect to be given an immunization record with the first shot and then have it up-dated each time.

74. If a diagnosis has been made on your child with which you are not comfortable, it is wise to obtain a second opinion. If surgery needs to be performed, this is always a good idea. If a serious diagnosis has been made, you

want the best possible specialist to see your child. Specialists can be seen in other cities and if there are financial problems, some airlines have special programs where they will fly families to see a specialist in another city. American Airlines has been particularly good about this. A letter will be needed from your primary doctor to the airlines. If a child has a serious diagnosis, such as cancer, a muscle disease, or other disorders requiring a microscopic diagnosis after a muscle biopsy or lymph node removal, it is very important to have the pathology slides reviewed by a specialist in that disorder. There may or may not be a charge for this. Slides can be sent from the pathology lab to the specialist. This will require a letter of request from a parent with permission to send the material.

> Parents from out of state contacted me about their four-year-old because a neurologist in a medical school had said their child had muscular dystrophy. The pathologist who looked at the muscle biopsy agreed with this diagnosis.
>
> However, when the mother and father described the little girl's symptoms, these sounded more like dermatomyositis, which is a treatable muscle disease. On reviewing the muscle biopsy slides and examining the child, there was no question that she had dematomyositis. By working with her local pediatrician and treating her aggressively with steroids (cortisone), the child regained her muscle strength.

75. It is important to know what to expect from the doctor caring for your baby or child. An initial examination should include history of pregnancy, labor, Apgar score (See Appendix), family history, diet, daily activities, feeding, general behavior, sleeping habits, development, any problems, and toilet training in a little child. Height, weight, and head size are very important measurements in babies and children. Growth charts should be plotted to make sure a child is following his or her expected growth curve and head size. In addition, the following are important:

- An initial urine sample should be obtained and then checked <u>yearly.</u> This is to look for infection, sugar, blood, and protein.

- A tuberculin skin test should be given every two years and in high-risk states, such as California, every year.

- Hearing should be checked in a pediatric hearing center if no sounds are made by three months. Even if a newborn exam was okay, it should be repeated if there is any question. Only 38 states mandate that hearing be checked at birth, and there can always be mistakes.

- Immunization records should be checked at each visit and any necessary immunizations given.

19. Choosing an HMO or Health Insurance

76. If you decide to join an HMO for financial reasons, you need to understand how they function and to read all the rules and regulations before you sign up. Before deciding to join an HMO, check the following about the care for babies and children:

- Are well-baby or well-child examinations covered?

- Are immunizations covered?

- Can you change doctors if you are unhappy with the doctor assigned to care for your baby or child?

- Are prescriptions covered?

- Are birth defects covered for orthopedic or other specialist care?

- Are cochlear implants covered?

- Are surgeries covered?

- Can your child be seen by a specialist outside of the HMO?

- Is ER care covered?

- Is ER care covered in a hospital out-of-state?

- Are routine lab tests covered, as urinalysis and blood counts?

- Are X-Rays, CT scans, or MRIs covered?

- Are you restricted as to what hospital you can use?

77. Because HMOs have a language of their own, it is important to learn what the different terms mean.

- **Gatekeepers** are the physicians who decide which doctors you can and cannot see, and determine which tests, procedures, or surgeries your child and family can and cannot have. The gatekeeper may be the physician assigned to your family or someone who knows nothing about you or your children. Many decisions are made by office staff or administrators, who have no medical training. Registered nurses are hired by some HMOs to make decisions and these frequently override a physician's recommendations. This has led to some tragic outcomes and major lawsuits.

- **IPA**-Independent Practice Association-This is a group of physicians who practice in their own offices, but agree to abide by the payment plan and regulations of the HMO. A physician is paid a specified amount of money for each patient in his or her care. This money is received whether or not the patient needs care. Children with birth defects, disabilities of any kind, or multiple health problems are not wanted by HMOs and their care may not be covered.

- **PPO**-Preferred Provider Organization-This is as group of physicians who have joined together. By becoming a member of their group, discounted fees will be received. If a patient is treated by an "outside" physician, a large part or the entire fee will be the responsibility of the patient or the parents. Referrals to an outside specialist may not be covered.

- **PCP**-Primary Care Physician-A physician who is responsible for your child's healthcare needs. He or she should make referrals to specialists as needed, but many of the doctors are reluctant to make referrals because this can reduce their pay. A "report card" is kept by many HMOs listing the number of referrals each physician makes. Referrals cost the HMO and physicians more, and thus are greatly discouraged.

- **Capitation**-This is the amount of money an HMO pays a physician for every patient he or she is expected to see. The doctor makes more money if the patients are not seen, tests are not requested, and referrals are not made to outside physicians.

- **Co-Payment**-This is the amount of money you are asked to pay at each office visit. The amount varies according to each individual plan.

- **Preadmission Certification**-All hospital admissions for surgery or medical care have to be pre-approved by a representative from the HMO or insurance company. Nurses do this in most cases, but your child's physician can insist on speaking with the medical director if approval is not given. The doctor's office staff or the physician should arrange for the hospital admission.

78. If you plan to enroll in an HMO or take out health insurance, be sure to check which physicians your child will be able to see. You may think that the physician you have been using is covered and belatedly discover that he or she is not part of the HMO, or covered by that insurance company. If your child is going to need to see outside specialists, be sure their visits are covered. You should not rely on verbal communication, *but get everything in writing prior to enrolling and the name of the individual or individuals who help you.*

> A family with limited financial resources signed up for medical care in an HMO. Their new baby was born with joints that would not move. The HMO did not have a doctor with training to treat the child. In addition, medical coverage for the baby was denied. When a specialist called the Medical Director of the HMO about covering the child's medical expenses, the doctor said, "We are not responsible for the care of a disabled child. That is up to the school or the community!"

Trying to save money by joining an HMO or using a particular insurance company may be one of the worst decisions you ever make. HMOs and insurance companies rarely allow referrals to outside specialists. Their decision can be appealed, but this takes a great deal of time and energy. Most parents do not have the time or energy to do this and often have to pay for the needed specialist themselves.

79. First and Second-level appeals can be filed if a needed test, procedure, hospitalization, or specialist is not granted. To do this you need to check the HMO rules and regulations to see how long you have to file an appeal. It is usually between 30 to 60 days. Save every medical and hospital bills you have received if you have to go ahead for a treatment or hospitalization for your child. Keep a record also of all the telephone conversations and correspondence you have had with HMO or insurance personnel. If a first-level appeal is denied try to find out the name of the individual who denied it. If both first and second-level appeals have been denied, you can often get a favorable outcome if you *state in a letter to the Medical Director that you are willing to contact an attorney.* Some large lawsuits have been filed against HMOs and insurance companies costing them large sums of money. Thus, your willingness to consult an attorney may make all the difference in having your child's bills paid.

20. Handling Relatives and Friends

80. It is important to establish right from the minute your baby is born that you, as the parents, are the experts with your child.

A new mother sat in my office on the verge of tears. "My mother," she said, "came to help me with the baby, but she is driving me crazy. She has always been into micromanagement and now she is managing me and my child. I love my mother very much and she means well, but she is undermining my role as the baby's mother. She doesn't listen and thinks she knows better than I do. What can I do?"

I said there is a generational difference in raising children and my suggestions were:

- Try not to get into a power struggle.

- Stick to what you know is best for your baby.

- Say "I know what I'm talking about."

- Be assertive, such as "I know the baby just needs a nap."

- Offer suggestions as "This would be helpful."

- Try to head a parent off "at the pass."

- Say you can recognize your baby's different cries. They are not all the same. A cry may mean a bubble, a B.M, tiredness, the need for a hug or that the baby is "wired".

- Explain your feelings and say you appreciate his or her efforts, but please let me do it my way.

A problem that can develop with grandparents is when parents want them involved, and they seem uninterested.

A new mother seemed distraught when we sat in my office after I had examined her baby. I assured her that Marcia was healthy and doing well and then said, "I sense something else is bothering you. "Well," the mother admitted, "I had hoped my parents would be available to baby-sit, but they don't offer and they seem to want to keep their distance from Marcia." When I asked if she had talked to her parents about this she said, "They say they are very busy and are planning on doing lots of traveling. I guess since they have already raised five children maybe they are tired. I hope we at least get to see them for a holiday now and then. My husband's parents live in Europe, so that means Marcia won't get to really know any of her grandparents."

Grandparents can be over involved or under involved, and as parents you may have to figure out ways to work around both problems. There may be an older woman who would love to fill in as a substitute grandparent. When I was in private pediatric practice and often called out at night, we had a wonderful woman, a former teacher, live with us to help with the children. She became a much-loved substitute grandparent "Sparksy," as the children called her, played an important part in my children's lives.

Section III

Children

21. Allergies

81. Allergies can range from food intolerance to eczema, hay fever, or asthma. Some migraine headaches may be due to allergies. Cow's milk is a common offender in little children and should be eliminated if allergic problems start to develop. The most important thing parents can do for an allergic child is to see a good pediatric allergist. A pediatric dermatologist should be seen for eczema and a hospital nutritionist can help with highly allergic babies. Many foods have additives that can cause problems in allergic babies and children.

> I was amazed and horrified when, at a pediatric clinical rounds, a pediatric allergist presented five children who had had severe asthma. None of the kids had been seen by a pediatric allergist once their asthma started and all were later found by the presenting doctor to be allergic to milk. Once all milk products were stopped, the kids no longer had asthma. I was sad that the parents and children had had to go through so many scary days. Asthma can have very serious consequences if it is not adequately treated or prevented.

82. Parents who have severely allergic children should always have an EpiPen at home, in the car and at a child's school or preschool. An EpiPen is a handy single dose of adrenalin or epinephrine that should be used when a severe allergic reaction occurs. Grandparents, too, should have EpiPens available if an allergic grandchild visits them from time to time. It is wise to practice with an EpiPen, so you will feel comfortable using it, if it might be needed. An orange or grapefruit is a good object to practice on and a nurse in the doctor's office should be able to help if you are uncomfortable about using an EpiPen. Peanuts can be a particular problem and some schools are banning peanut butter sandwiches if a highly allergic child attends. All parents with a highly allergic child should have an emergency plan that the schools, family friends, relatives, and babysitters all know. The American College of Allergy, Asthma and Immunology can be reached at 1-847-427-1200 or **www.acaai.org**.

83. A good pediatric allergist should give you a list or brochure about how to allergy-proof your house. Some children are very sensitive to dust mites, but much can be done to keep a child's room and the house as dust-free as possible. Having special allergy-free mattresses, pillows (not feather-filled), cotton blankets and rugs are all important. Frequent cleaning of the house and washing of bed clothes is also important. The yard can be a source of allergens: dust, grasses, weeds, mold, oak, elm, pecan, and maple trees. All bother some children. In Rochester, New York school was delayed in opening when the pollen count was too high and the pollen count was published daily in the paper. Animals, too, can cause allergic reactions in some children. Dogs and cats are often the culprits. Cigarette smoke can be very hard on some allergic children. To screen out pollens and allergens, air conditioners or dehumidifiers may be needed. Allergy injections can make a great difference for some kids. Fortunately, many children outgrow their allergies.

Many years ago, I had a cute little boy as a patient who had frequent asthma attacks. I wanted the child to see a good pediatric allergist, but it took the mother a long time to make the appointment. Finally, with a lot of pressure from me, the appointment was made and allergy testing completed. The results showed the primary allergen to be cigarette smoke. I knew the mother was a chain smoker and when I gave her the results of the tests, she said, "Well, Michael can just have his asthma, because I am not going to stop smoking." I was horrified, but couldn't convince the woman to even smoke outside the house. She was extremely wealthy and spoiled and I had no way to make her stop smoking. I was glad when the family moved away because I felt powerless about helping the sweet little boy. Yes, there are parents who put their own needs above those of their children's. If your child is allergic, a neighbor or friend should know to follow any restrictions if your child spends time with them.

22. Feeding

84. Young children usually eat what they need, unless they fill up on milk or snacks between meals. 2-year-olds often prefer milk to food and can develop a milk anemia due to lack of iron and good protein. Constipation can also become a problem if milk is the primary food. Some small children are very picky eaters, particularly if they aren't expected to eat what is put in front of them, but are always fixed special treats or the foods they like.

Tony, a three-year-old, was making life very difficult for his parents because he liked few foods and would have a temper tantrum if he didn't get exactly what he wanted.

When asked for my advice, I suggested putting small, attractive portions of food in front of Tony and if he started to have temper tantrums to get him down from the table. I urged the mother to call me if she and her husband were finding it too difficult to follow this plan.

For the next four days, I had a daily distress call from the mother, but urged her to wait a little while longer. As long as Tony was urinating and eating something, he wasn't going to starve. Finally, on the fifth day, the mother called saying, "Tony is eating us out of house and home." After that there were no problems.

---

85. Small children usually like simple, single foods. Other tips about feeding little children are:

- Mixtures, such as casseroles, are not readily accepted.

- Eating meals with a child helps if they are poor eaters.

- Having a regular meal-time makes a difference and also allows important family time together.

- If a particular food is disliked, a child may be allergic to it.

- A child should not be forced to eat everything on the plate.

- Snacks between meals are not wise for children with small appetites. Apple juice is a good between meal snack.

- Graham crackers contain much sugar and should be given as a treat only now and then.

- For preemies or underweight children, small meals and frequent high protein snacks may be needed.

- Candy, cookies, and ice cream should be given just as special treats.

- Milk between meals will diminish a child's appetite for meals.

- Apples and bananas should be avoided for constipated kids.

- Start one new food at a time, so an allergy can be detected.

- Vegetarian diets can lack greatly in protein unless great care is taken. I would make a list of all the foods eaten for a few days, and check the list with your doctor or a dietician.

- Pre-packaged children's food may contain lots of calories and may not provide the best nutrition. Read the ingredients before buying these.

86. Obesity in children has become a major concern in the U.S. Children usually follow the eating habits of their parents. If fatty, greasy foods fast foods, pre-packaged meals and high-caloric snacks are the family norm, obesity can become a major problem for all family members. Instead, if children become accustomed to high protein, fiber-containing foods at an early age, they will be much better off. Obesity can lead to diabetes, increased blood pressure (hypertension), and heart disease. Also, obese children can be teased unmercifully by other children. Adequate amounts of exercise are extremely important for obese kids, as is true for all kids. It is also important for the parent or individual doing the food shopping to read labels and see what ingredients are included. Many soft drinks include caffeine and high caloric fructose corn syrup is present in many foods. If a child spends time at a baby-sitter's or relative's house, parents need to be sure that lots of high-calorie sweets are not being offered.

I had a patient with a muscle disorder who was rapidly gaining weight. When I asked his mother how much exercise Roger got. She replied, "Almost none." Then when I asked how much TV he watched, the mother said "About six hours a day!" No wonder the boy was gaining weight. I suggested the family buy a stationary bicycle and that Roger could only be allowed to watch TV when he was using the bicycle (Often, these bicycles can be purchased second-hand.)

23. Toilet Training

87. Every child has a time when he or she is ready for toilet training. If parents make toilet training a control issue and insist that their children be trained before their nervous systems are mature enough, temper tantrums, soiling and other problems may develop. No child is ready to be toilet trained before walking begins, and usually not until several months later. (Girls are generally ready for toilet training before boys.) A little child should always show interest before toilet training will be successful or should be started.

I was in a San Francisco coffee shop one day and overheard two women at the next table discussing their children's toilet training. One woman was bragging that her child was trained before a year of age, while the other mother said, "Sam is almost three and he still isn't completely trained. He seems afraid of the potty." I felt sad for the first mother anticipating that before too many years, her child might start rebelling at what I suspected was an overly controlling mother.

88. A child's small potty should be placed in the bathroom and when a child indicates readiness, he or she should be placed on it at a regular time after a meal. Some little children feel more secure with side-rails on their potty seat. If any resistance or unhappiness occurs, I would not put a child on the potty for a few weeks. Marked constipation can cause soiling and delay training. A crack or fissure next to the rectum can cause painful bowel movements, so a child will want to hold them back.

24. Discipline

89. It is hard for some parents to discipline children because they think it is punishment. Many parents these days no longer seem to be able to say "No" and mean it; instead the vogue seems to be to give a child choices, when instead they need and want boundaries. By establishing rules and sticking to them, children know what to expect and will feel secure. Otherwise, they can become quite anxious.

It is hard to be consistent, and kids are very smart about trying to manipulate or "con" parents. They start this at an early age and are good about trying to play one parent against the other. When parents don't act like adults, but try to be their child's "friends", trouble lies ahead. Kids want their parents in control. They are too young to be in-charge of a family, and if they are great anxiety can result. (I've had older children tell me they wish their parents would make rules and stick by them, because then they would know what is expected of them.) Parents need to be able to say "**No**" and mean it.

At a parents' seminar on discipline, a tall, imposing father said he and his wife were having great trouble disciplining their two-year-old boy. The child had temper tantrums, threw things, and was always whining. When I asked if he and his wife tried to use the same rules and be consistent, the father answered sheepishly, "Well, I guess we have trouble with that." My answer was, "It seems as if your son is running the family and at age two, he is pretty young to be in-charge." The father answered, "I'm afraid you are right. I guess we need to work together and be more consistent." When I called two weeks later, things were better and the little boy and his parents were much happier.

90. Temper tantrums and breath-holding spells are usually attention-seeking mechanisms. If kids are ignored or put in their rooms, the tantrums and breath-holding will stop, unless there is a serious problem. Some good tips for disciplining are:

- Discipline should be individualized and age-appropriate. A little child who is having a temper tantrums may need to be put in his or her room or ignored until the tantrum stops. Another child may respond to a stern look and a strong "**No**".

- When you say "No", mean it and stick to it unless you are wrong.

- Losing control and yelling or disciplining in anger can cause physical and emotional harm.

- Never hit or strike a child in anger or otherwise.

- A *parent's voice* should be the best means of control.

- As kids get older, they can help work out fair rules. Usually it is best to give kids just two choices. They don't' do well with many choices.

- If you have lost control or been too harsh, go ahead and say "I'm sorry". No parent can always be in control and without fault.

- Always praise good behavior instead of criticizing or commenting just on bad behavior.

25. Safety

91. Keeping children safe is quite easy when they are infants, but can get harder as they become crawlers and begin to explore. Some basic things parents can do to ensure as much safety as possible is a good safety inspection before a child begins to crawl. This should include:

- Covering outlets with special covers you can buy.

- Checking for any open wires or frayed cords.

- Putting a guard or screen around a wall furnace and fireplace.

- Checking that toys don't have removable eyes, buttons, or detachable parts.

- Putting all medicines under lock and key. (Check bedside table drawers or headboards.)

- Putting cleaning supplies and dishwasher soap up high.

- Getting rid of poisonous plants.

- Never leaving plastic bags where a little child can reach them.

- Having adequate smoke and carbon monoxide detectors. These can be connected electronically, so if there is a fire in one area all the smoke detectors will be set off.

- Keeping matches, electric cords, and appliances out of a child's reach.

- Turning down the water heater temperature if it is over 120 degrees Fahrenheit.

- Keeping pot handles turned away from the edge of the stove.

- Having safety gates at the top and bottom of stairs.

- Using a playpen when you are busy.

- Doing a safety inspection before going to bed each night to check for small objects: beads, coins, or pins.

- Always keeping cigarettes, cigarette butts, and alcohol out of a child's reach.

- Keeping a small child out of the garage. There are usually many poisons and dangerous tools around.

- Being sure windows and screens are closed or have special locks to keep a child from slipping out. (This is particularly important for children with autism, who like to escape.)

- Putting visiting women's purses up high. They may contain medicine or small objects that can be swallowed.

- Removing toy chests lids that can fall on a child's head or catch hands.

- Not using mothballs or buying candy that looks like mothballs.

- Making washing machines and dryers off-limits.

- Discarding old refrigerators and trunks in a safe place and being sure they are tightly locked.

- Surrounding swimming pools by a fence and making them off-limits. A pool cover can be dangerous, if a small child can slip under it. Fish ponds can also be lethal. If a child is in a swimming pool, a responsible adult, not a teenager, must always be present and attentive at poolside.

- Putting burning candles out of reach of little ones.

- Removing scissors, razor blades, and sharp knives from places where a small child can reach them.

- Putting cosmetics, perfumes, hair dyes and bleaches, and nail polish and removers all up high.

- Making sure garden supplies, insecticides, sprays, snail, slug, and rat poisons are not where a small child can reach them.

- Covering sharp corners on furniture.

- Locking guns up in a cupboard with the key carefully hidden. *(Guns should never be left loaded.)*

- Be sure that relatives and friends where your children play do not have accessible guns.

- Insist that children wear helmets if they are on a tricycle, scooter, and skateboard or have had a head injury.

- Keeping a small child from pulling a table cloth off of a table when the table is set for a meal or has lighted candles on it.

- Having someone supervise a small child on moving day.

- Dinner time, too, is often a dangerous time if a little one is not watched. With several people in your house at a party, it may be easy for a little child to slip out.

92. The numbers for the local and national poison centers should be posted by your principal phone or all phones. The National Poison Center number is 1-800-222-1222. All parents, relatives who babysit, and caretakers should know CPR for kids. Syrup of Ipecac is no longer recommended when a poisonous substance has been ingested. Instead, the poison center and your child's doctor should be called and the child taken to the nearest emergency room. The poisonous substance or plant should be taken along, so the ER personnel will know what they are treating.

93. Little children can choke easily. There are several foods to be avoided: hard candies, nuts, popcorn, peanut butter chunks, raw vegetables, and whole grapes, chunks of meat or cheese, and hot dogs. Children should be sitting down when

they are eating and not running or walking with food in their mouth. Toys with detachable parts or pacifiers that pull apart can cause choking. Latex balloons and plastic bags can also cause choking.

The new fad with some parents to give their children a diet of raw food can be dangerous. One mother, who didn't like to cook, but had plenty of free time, gave her two small children hunks of raw vegetables to eat. The two-year-old could not chew these well and had to be taken by ambulance to the local Children's Hospital. He had a large piece of broccoli in his lungs, which had to be surgically removed. Even though the child could have died, the mother continued feeding the two little children chunks of raw vegetables.

94. Children's toys and products that are recalled can be reviewed at the U.S. Consumer Product Safety Commission Web site, www.cpsc.gov. The toll-free number is: 1-800-638-2772. The agency will also send free safety and consumer information.

95. Never leave a baby or child alone in a car, particularly on a hot day. Always carry an extra set of keys, in case you lock your keys in the car.

A mother dashed frantically into a small grocery store saying she had locked her keys and her baby in the car. It was a record hot day, so someone immediately called 911. Other people ran to help the mother try to unlock the car. Fortunately, the father was still at home and hurried to the rescue. Other parents have not been as fortunate, and periodically there is a newspaper account of a child who died when locked in a car on a hot day.

26. Daycare Tips

96. Choosing the right daycare for a little one is an important decision. The wrong daycare can be a source of multiple infections, accidents, and even contagious diseases. Networking with other parents, asking your child's doctor, and looking at parents' newsletters or local parent magazines will give you an idea about what is available. Some good steps to take are:

- Ask if a daycare center is accredited and the number of adults per child.
- Talk to several parents with children enrolled in the daycare you like.
- Find out daily routines, as to naps, eating, and playtime.
- Ask if sick children are sent home or kept isolated.
- Find out how close is the nearest emergency room, doctor, or hospital.
- Inquire if the staff have yearly TB tests or chest X-rays.
- Check to see if the staff members have emergency or CPR training.
- Ask about staff backgrounds, references, and finger printing.
- Drop in unexpectedly and see if the kids are happy and clean.
- Find out how long the center has been in business.

There are two good resources to find out about daycare centers. The National Association of Child Care Resource and Referral Agencies at 1-202-393-5501, and National Child Care Association at 1-800-543-7161.

> A mother carefully checked out a daycare center for her three-year-old and for a while everything went well. Then one day she called frantically saying the little boy had swallowed some dishwasher detergent he had found under a sink. Fortunately, he spit it out, so no bad burns resulted, as could have happened.

27. Hospitalizations

97. Hospitals can be frightening places, even if you are part of a family with doctors or a medical professional. If you have to spend time in a hospital with a child, because of illness, surgery or a broken bone, it is important to know some of the pitfalls and ways to prevent problems.

- Check if you need a pre-authorization from your insurance company or HMO before an admission.

- Ask the names of the nurses and other staff members and use them.

- Always have a parent, relative, or friend stay with a child.

- Don't let anyone intimidate you.

- *Insist that your child's doctor visit and speak with you daily.*

- Be sure your child has a favorite blanket or stuffed animal.

- If you are not happy with the care, speak up.

- Always seek a second medical opinion if you are not comfortable with the medical care or treatment.

- Don't overwhelm a child with gifts or toys.

- Don't be afraid to speak to the head of the hospital if a major problem develops.

- Check the hospital bill carefully.

- If the care is unsatisfactory even after you have complained to the CEO, then, if possible, take your child to a different hospital.

- If a surgery is planned, take a small child to visit the hospital prior to the date. Playing doctor or nurse with masks and caps is fun and helps. There are also good books for kids about hospital stays.

A diabetic child was sent in the early afternoon to the pediatric ward of a local hospital by the child's pediatrician. By 7 that evening, the doctor had not telephoned orders for the child, nor seen him. Fortunately, the parents knew this was dangerous and took the boy to a Children's Hospital about 30 miles away. The next week, the other pediatricians voted to remove the doctor from their staff. The diabetic child had been extremely ill with a very high blood sugar and by moving their son to another hospital, the parents probably prevented him from going into a diabetic coma.

28. Adoptions

98. When adoption is considered, parents are faced with many questions. Should they seek a child by private adoption, from foster care, or overseas? Some parents are willing to adopt a special needs child and find this role fulfilling. This is not for everyone, but there are some lovely kids waiting to be adopted. Some basic tips about adoption are:

- Be sure a reputable lawyer is involved if the adoption is private.

- Do your homework about adoptions.

- Have a child carefully checked by a pediatrician.

- Be sure a tuberculin test, blood count, and urinalysis are done initially, plus any other needed tests.

- Children from overseas need multiple screening tests.

- Don't wait too long to let a child know he or she is adopted.

A professional man stopped me one day to ask when he and his wife should tell their fifteen-year-old son that he was adopted. "You mean he doesn't know?" I asked. I knew there was another son who the father said was not adopted. I suggested that the sooner the youth knew the better it would be. It had been much too long, as far as I was concerned and I felt it would come as a great shock to the fifteen-year-old.

- Find out as much about the child's family history as possible.

- Adopted children do have a higher incidence of learning and other difficulties.

- Before adopting a child, if you have not spent much time with kids, offer to babysit a friend's child to be sure adoption is what you want to do.

- Children from overseas should always have an opportunity to learn about their cultures.

A good friend who was adopted as a baby told me what an impact being adopted has had on her life. She has always had a terrible fear of abandonment and though she has been married and had a rich life, she says being by herself makes her uncomfortable and feel abandoned. She did find the name of her birth mother, but because the woman was no longer living, there was never an answer about why she had been put up for adoption.

> One family adopted a 2-year-old, but after many sleepless nights and multiple problems with the child, the parents finally decided they could no longer cope. The child's problems were tearing them apart, and they feared for their marriage. It took great courage for them to say they could no longer handle the child and returned him to the adoption agency.

Some good resources are:

National Adoption Clearinghouse
www.adoption.org/adopt/national-adoption-clearing-house

Adopt a Special Kid **www.aask.org**
Joint Council on International Children's Services at **www.jcics.org**

29. Health Concerns

99. **All children should see a pediatrician or family doctor regularly.** Alternative medicine has a place for adults, but can be risky for babies and children. Children are not little adults. Some good rules to follow are:

- <u>Never</u> give herbal medicines to kids. Deaths have occurred.
- Give babies and children a daily multi-vitamin, unless they drink vitamin-fortified milk. Health store vitamins should not be given.
- Have vision and hearing checked yearly or if there seems to be a problem.
- Have urine checked yearly for infection, blood, sugar, or protein or if there is a fever for which the cause cannot be found.
- Be sure kids drink adequate water and not just juice or soft drinks.
- Put sunscreen and hats on children when outdoors on warm days.
- Babies under six months should <u>not</u> have sunscreen lotion applied.
- Be sure children wash their hands after playing with pets.
- Be sure pets receive all their shots.
- Keep a first-aid kit at home and in the car.
- *Insist* the doctor listens if you have a health concern about a child.
- Dental care is extremely important for kids, as is brushing their teeth. A regular routine should be established as soon as possible for children when they are old enough to brush their own teeth.

One stepmother of a teenager with a disability was giving the girl twenty-two different herbal medicines. These ruined the girl's appetite and she was losing weight that she could not afford to lose. Once the herbal medicines were stopped, the girl's appetite gradually returned. Another parent was giving her child medicines from a Chinese herbalist. When I called an M.D. who was knowledgeable about these medicines, he was horrified. Most of them he said were only for adults and one could cause convulsions or seizures in a child. Fortunately, the father and grandparents intervened, and the herbal medicines were destroyed.

30. Single Parenting

100. The problems of being a single parent are different if you are a divorced parent or a single mother by choice. If you are raising a child alone, you can parent the way you feel is right without having to talk to a partner. The minus side of being a single parent is that the responsibility is all yours and there is no partner with whom to discuss your concerns and share the load. It can be a lonely road, if you try to do it all without help. Many divorced parents still communicate about their children, and this is best for the kids. If you are raising a child alone, either as a mother or father, it is important to establish a good support system. There will always be a time when you will need another pair of hands or someone to do an errand. Big Brothers and Big Sisters do a great job of providing someone to spend time with a child. Other parents are a good resource, as are senior citizens, grandparents, and teenagers.

101. There are several do's and don'ts for being a single parent:

- Don't try to be a super-parent.
- Find a reliable babysitter.
- Develop a support system.
- Ask for help when you need it.
- Find a mothers' or fathers' support group.
- Find an online chat group if you enjoy this type of interaction.
- Take care of yourself with some weekly exercise and a good diet.

- Don't have your child sleep with you.
- Be a parent, not your child's best friend.
- Interact with other families, as well as single parents.
- Parents Without Partners is a resource.
- Don't spoil your child with too many toys or other things.
- Don't be afraid to establish rules and stick to them.

I flew to a big conference with a well-known celebrity. She was giving a talk at noon, and I was giving a seminar. The woman, a single parent, told me how upset her adopted four-year-old had been when she left that morning. After giving talks, while we were waiting to board our flight home, the celebrity went to the airport gift shop and came back with a bag of candy and toys. I looked at her and said, "You are going to be in my next book." The woman was not amused and said "What do you mean?" What I meant was I felt the mother was trying to buy her little girl with gifts, rather than spending time with her. I knew the woman, as a TV celebrity, was gone from home a great deal of the time.

SINGLE MOTHERS

I have found that single mothers often try to make their sons act as the "man or men" of the family. One mother even slept with her son and tried to control his choice of friends. When the boy got older and started to break away from his mother's control, she came to me with tears in her eyes. Eventually, the youth left home, and it broke the mother's heart

SINGLE FATHERS

When a father receives full custody of the children, which happens more and more, the man should be particularly careful about his relationship with his daughter or daughters.

Many mothers and fathers are uncomfortable about having a daughter play at the home of a single father when no other adult is present. Sleepovers with several little girls are times to be particularly careful. It is wise to have a grandmother or older woman spend the night, so that there can never be any cause for parents to be concerned about their daughters' safety. Even though parents know the father quite well, it is always wise to be careful where little girls are concerned.

Conclusion

I hope my suggestions and advice will make parenting for each reader less stressful, and more fun. To me, a child is like a beautiful piece of art to be cherished and loved, but if your days are filled with too many activities, too much to do, and much stress, you will miss the wonderful moments of happiness and joy that children can bring. You will have good days and bad days, but I hope you will find time to celebrate the special times. A parent, who lost her much loved son at age 15 to Duchenne muscular dystrophy told me that "moments of happiness are like beads on a necklace. They can be strung together and always remembered and enjoyed." I hope each of you will find your own "Beads of Happiness," as you raise your children.

Appendix I
Questions & Answers

Question: Our 3-week-old baby boy has started vomiting about thirty minutes after he eats. He isn't gaining weight and his father and I are very worried. The doctor has given us some drops, but they don't seem to help. What do you suggest?

Answer: I would be concerned that your son has developed pyloric stenosis and would insist a pediatric surgeon see him right away. For some reason, usually in first-born male babies, a thickening develops at the end of the stomach (pylorus) that doesn't allow food to go through. This has to be corrected surgically, but it is a simple procedure.

2. Question: Our baby was born with a club foot, but our pediatrician doesn't think anything needs to be done right away. We don't want to wait, if there is something that should be done right now.

Answer: Your baby should be seen right away by a pediatric orthopedic surgeon. A general orthopedist is not the doctor you want. If you belong to an HMO, and there is not a pediatric orthopedist in the group, I would insist on an outside referral. If this is not possible and you don't want to file a first-level appeal, I would seek a consultation at the nearest Shriner's Hospital.

3. Question: Our 1-year-old little girl has large, greasy-looking stools. Our family doctor doesn't seem to know what to do or isn't concerned. What should we do?

Answer: The diagnosis of Celiac disease should be considered when there are fatty, greasy stools. A pediatric gastroenterologist needs to be seen. This is a treatable disorder due to wheat, oat, and rye intolerance. The Celiac Foundation will send literature and there are cookbooks for celiac disease meals. The telephone number is 1-818-990-2354 and their website is **www.celiac.org**.

4. Question: Our 4-month-old little girl is not lifting up her head, rolling over or moving very much. She is very alert and bright-eyed, but seems to be getting weaker and weaker. Our pediatrician has done several tests but doesn't know what the problem is. What specialist should we see?

Answer: It sounds as though your baby girl could have a neuromuscular disorder. It would be important to see a pediatric neuromuscular specialist. Unfortunately, there are very few in the United States, so you may have to travel some distance, as for example to the Mayo Clinic in Minnesota.

5. Question: Our 3-month-old little boy has an enormous appetite and seems hard to fill up. He is both breast and bottle-fed. Do you have any suggestions?

Answer: In general, it is recommended that solid foods be started about six months. However, in caring for many, many babies, I have found that there are some babies who cannot be filled-up with just milk. Adding a little rice cereal in one or two bottles helps. I've used this method to great advantage in countless babies and my own son. It was life-saving! Thickened formulas can also help prevent spitting-up.

6. Question: Our baby has a mass or hernia protruding at the navel. Our doctor says not to worry about it. Is he right?

Answer: Umbilical hernias are quite common in babies. Most of them will go away or resolve by eighteen months. If you continue to worry, I would make an appointment with a pediatric surgeon.

7. Question: Our 2-year-old's grandparents keep buying expensive toys and clothes. We don't want to hurt their feelings, but Rick is getting spoiled and being given too much. How can we handle this?

Answer: I would set the stage and talk to the grandparents when they are relaxed and comfortable, such as after a good dinner. First, I would thank them for all they have done for your child, but then gently request they not be so lavish with their gifts. You might suggest they need to use the money for treats for themselves. If this doesn't work, then I would put the new toys or gifts away for a while and bring them out one at a time over a period of days or weeks.

8. Question: Our little 2-year-old hates vegetables. He will eat meat and fruit, but that is all. Do you have any suggestions?

Answer: You can put vegetables through a blender and add them to foods he likes. This may or may not work. I would keep trying, but as long as he is a good eater otherwise and getting a multi-vitamin, he should be o.k. Some children take longer than others to eat vegetables. I would not force him to eat them. Some kids who do not like most vegetables will eat a baked potato or beans. Both are good foods.

9. Question: Our little girl loves milk and gets very constipated. What do you suggest? We have tried to limit the amount of milk she drinks, but it is still her favorite food.

Answer: First, I would dilute any milk you give your daughter and offer milk only after meals. Then I would give her apricot nectar between meals and add bran flakes to her cereal or other foods. Most kids also like bran muffins. Remember that apples and bananas are constipating.

10. Question: Our 3-year-old is autistic and we are having a problem with him when he is put down for a nap. He pulls down his diapers and smears poop all around. What do you suggest?

Answer: I would suggest putting soft splints around both elbows, so he can't bend his arms during naptime. You could use a stiff cardboard or even a small magazine wrapped with an ace bandage. Feces can cause illness, so your child needs to learn this is not a good thing to do.

11. Question: Our 2-year-old has started limping. The doctor thinks it is a sprained ankle, but there isn't any swelling. Jake doesn't want to put weight on his foot. No X-ray has been taken.

Answer: I would insist that an X-ray be taken of the ankle and foot. I had one patient who had a needle in his foot that was causing a limp. If the X-ray is negative then I would make an appointment with a pediatric orthopedic surgeon. There could be a problem in the hip joint. If the orthopedist can't find the cause of the limp, then I would want to have a blood count and sedimentation rate done. There could be a more serious problem that a pediatric oncologist (a cancer doctor) should investigate.

12. Question: Our 18-month-old has had pus coming from his ear for almost three weeks. The doctor keeps giving us antibiotics, but it is not getting better. What should we do?

Answer: I wouldn't be surprised if your child has put something in his ear canal. It needs to be cleaned out to see if there is a foreign body there. Then the ear drum can be seen. If your doctor doesn't want to do this, I would see a children's ear-nose-throat doctor. I've removed strange objects from little kids' ear canals. The pus will not go away until the foreign body is removed.

13. Question: When I clean the bathroom, I notice that the floor around the toilet is sticky and smelly. I know our little boy often misses the toilet bowl. Do you think something is wrong?

Answer: I would urge you to take a urine specimen to your doctor or to the lab he or she suggests. The urine should be checked for infection, protein, blood, and sugar. Diabetes is a real possibility, particularly if any family members have diabetes.

14. Question: Our 2-year-old little girl has pus coming out between her legs. The doctor has given us some salve and we keep her very clean. It doesn't seem to be getting any better. What else can we do?

Answer: I would want to be sure your child has not put a foreign object into her vagina. This is quite common in little girls. The doctor needs to do a rectal to see if anything can be felt. An X-ray of the lower part of the abdomen may also show an object, if it is metal.

15. Question: Our little girl often angrily throws food on the floor, if she doesn't like something we put on her plate. We don't know how to handle this. Can you help?

Answer: I would very calmly take your child down from the table and put her in her room. Then, I would not offer any food until the next meal. If you do this each time it happens, she will soon get hungry enough to stop misbehaving.

16. Question: Our 2-week-old little girl had a hard time arriving. Now she has a firm nodule in the muscle in the front of the neck. The doctor doesn't seem worried, but we need more information about why it is there and what we should do.

Answer: Babies who have a hard delivery or a breech delivery sometimes have bleeding into the muscle at the front of the neck. This is the sternocleidomastoid muscle. Usually, the nodule goes away, but sometimes it leads to torticollis or twisting of the neck. If this occurs, it is important to gently move the baby's head to the other side a few times a day and put a mobile on that side of the crib, so she needs to turn her head toward it. In most cases, this is all that is necessary but if the nodule persists, you may want to see a pediatric surgeon.

17. Question: Our little 2-month-old, Patsy, usually has a bowel movement every one to two days. Now she hasn't had one for five days and cries a lot. Our pediatrician says not to worry. What do you think?

Answer: I'm wondering if Patsy is getting enough water or juice. You could try a little dilute apple or prune juice. You could also insert half of an infant glycerin suppository into her rectum or anus to see if that would stimulate a bowel movement. If you are nursing, I suspect both you and Patsy need more fluids. Too little fluid can lead to constipation. Don't wait too long before Patsy has a bowel movement, and be sure the doctor does a rectal examination.

18. Question: Our baby has a red mark at the base of her neck below the hairline. Why did this happen and should we do anything about it?

Answer: This red mark is a very common finding in babies. Many lay people in the past called it a "stork-bite." There is nothing to do and it may fade. Some remain and are not a problem.

19. Question: Our 3-year-old little girl has started scratching between her legs. The doctor gave us some ointment to put on and we give her a daily bath. Neither of these seem to help. What do you suggest?

Answer: I would look for three things. First, I would be sure you are using a gentle soap, not a detergent, to watch your little girl's clothes. I would not use bubble bath and would suggest a soap, such as ivory. The third thing I would do is to go in after your child is asleep at night and using a flashlight look around her anus or rectum. Pinworms come out a night and can usually be seen with a flashlight. Fifty percent of small children have pinworms at some time and they pass them around. Pinworms can cause considerable itching. If you see little wiggly pinworms, your doctor can prescribe medicine. You will need to wash your child's sheets a little more frequently for a while.

20. Question: Our 2-year-old, Boyd, is "pigeon-toed." Our family doctor does not seem worried, but we are. My parents say he needs corrective shoes. What do you suggest?

Answer: Your little boy may need corrective shoes when he gets older, but if the toeing-in is mild probably nothing needs to be done at this time. To keep your parents from pestering you, an appointment with a children's orthopedic surgeon would be a good idea. Remember that mild bowing of the legs in a two-year-old is normal and the toeing-in may reflect a family pattern. It might be that you or the baby's father toed-in when you were little.

21. Question: My little boy loved going to school until the last few weeks. Now I have to force him to go. He won't tell me that anything is wrong, and I don't know what to do. I've tried to talk to his doctor, but she is young and doesn't seem interested. I've also talked with his teacher, but she doesn't seem to have a clue about what is going on with Tommy. What should I do?

Answer: I am wondering if Tommy is being bullied. It might be a good idea if you could volunteer for playground duty one day or help for a day or two in his classroom. Also, if you could talk with some of his friends or their parents that could be helpful. I would also ask if Tommy comes home with torn clothes or any scratches or bruises. If none of these ideas help, a child psychologist might be able to talk with Tommy and find out what is going on. Sometimes, play therapy will give answers.

22. Question: Our 6-month-old boy is bright, alert, and constantly trying to stand alone. He loves moving around in a walker. I just took him to the pediatrician for this month's check-up and she said he was "developmentally delayed" because he doesn't yet roll over. How could he be "developmentally delayed"? My husband and I are devastated by her statement.

Answer: I am appalled that a pediatrician would make such a statement. Any baby that is eagerly moving around and trying to walk at six months is certainly not "developmentally delayed." Some babies skip different developmental steps. It sounds as though your pediatrician has not been in practice very long. I would urge you to find a different doctor.

23. Question: Our little 18-month-old boy has chubby feet that look flat. Should we buy special shoes or take him to see an orthopedist?

Answer: All eighteen-month-old children have flat feet. They look even flatter if the children are chubby. There is nothing to worry about at this time.

Sometimes, when kids get older a little arch support is needed in their shoes if their feet are flat or seem to roll over. If you are still worried in a year or so, you could make an appointment with a pediatric orthopedic surgeon.

24. Question: My wife insists that our children be fed a vegetarian diet. I am not a vegetarian and am concerned that they are not getting enough protein, vitamins or minerals. What do you suggest?

Answer: It is very difficult to be sure a child is getting a balanced diet if they are not given any animal protein. For example, Vitamin B12 is only found in foods of animal origin: liver, kidneys, meats, milk, most cheeses, most fish and shellfish. I would suggest keeping a daily food record for one to two weeks and then discussing the log with a dietician. A daily multi-vitamin would also be important. Another concern is that according to Dr. Henry Legere, a "child would need to eat anywhere from three to seven times as much non-meat protein to get the amount of protein found in a single serving of meat or cheese." Most little children cannot eat large servings at a time, so this is also a worrisome aspect of vegetarian diets for small children.

25. Question: My 6-month-old baby is always sick with ear infections or pneumonia. The doctor just keeps giving her antibiotics. What are we doing wrong?

Answer: It sounds as though you may need to change doctors for one thing. Then I would insist that a complete blood count be done to look for anemia. In addition, if the blood count is o.k. I would see a pediatric allergist. Your baby may be allergic to cow's milk or something else. If there is no anemia and no allergy, then the doctor needs to look at the baby's immune system by doing some blood work.

26. Question: Our 6-month-old little boy has had diarrhea and fever on and off for three weeks. I have taken him to three different doctors, and they say it is viral and to just keep giving him fluids. Is there anything else that needs to be done?

Answer: I am wondering if a urinalysis has been checked and a stool sent to the lab to be cultured and to look for ova and parasites. Also, there is frequently an association between ear infections and diarrhea. Because some pediatricians don't know how or won't take the time to clean out ear canals, I would make an appointment with a good pediatric ear doctor to be sure there is not an ear infection. I would ask too that a blood count be done to be sure your baby is not anemic. It is harder for an infant or child fight infections with a low blood count.

27. Question: My 2-year-old grandchild keeps getting staph infections. What do you suggest?

Answer: I suspect that someone, who is around the child frequently, is a staph carrier. Family members, a child-care person or anyone else who is near your grandchild should have their nose and throat cultured. Putting a little Neosporin or Bactoban ointment in the front of each nostril for two or three days helps to get rid of staph. Also, washing for a few days with Dial soap or phisohex often eradicates staph. You may also need to wash the sheets more often.

28. Question: A friend's child wasn't doing some significant things by nine months, but the doctor just waived if off. This greatly concerned my friend. Should she be concerned?

Answer: Whenever a parent feels that something is not right, despite what a doctor says, I would always get a second opinion.

29. Question: How resilient are babies? Sometimes I feel my son gets tired out if I do too many errands?

Answer: Every baby and child has only a certain amount of tolerance for errands and shopping. Many times in a grocery or other store, I've seen tired, whiny babies and children and wished the parent would take them home for a nap. Not all of us like to shop!

30. Question: We are going to go on a five-hour airplane trip with our fifteen-month-old and wonder if we should take a car seat. Are there rules about this?

Answer: I would check with the specific airline. The airlines don't seem to have rules about car seats, except that if you take one on onboard, it must be airline certified. (Not all of them are.)

31. Question: My baby's soft spot is still open at 15 months. The doctor doesn't seem concerned about this. Should I worry?

Answer: Soft spots can stay open that long, but I would want to be sure that your doctor measures your baby's head at each visit and plots it on a special head chart. Also, I would want to be sure that your baby is developmentally doing o.k. If there is any question about this, I would get a second opinion. Most soft spots will close by about one year, but this is variable.

32. Question: My child has been diagnosed with a seizure disorder and put on medication. Could you please tell me how to be prepared if he has a seizure?

Answer: You are very wise to be prepared if a seizure occurs. It may not last very long, but it is important with a seizure that a child be placed on a flat surface where no sharp objects are within reach. You want to be sure the child's airway is open and that no food is stuck in his or her throat. Having someone call 911, if it is a grand mal seizure is also wise.

33. Question: My 3-year-old seems to get more tired than other children his age. His doctor doesn't seem concerned, but I feel that something is not right.

Answer: I would want a complete blood count or CBC and a urinalysis. Also it would be important to be sure your little boy is getting enough protein. Does your doctor ever ask what he is eating? By keeping a three-day record of everything he eats you will have an idea about something that may be missing.

Appendix II
Parent Resources

Helpful Websites

- www.nannycare.com
- www.parenthood.com
- www.babyzone.com
- www.parentplace.com
- www.positiveparenting.com
- www.parentime.com
- www.parentpals.com
- www.parenting.com
- www.zerotothree.org

Premature Infants

- www.preemiestoday.org
- www.premature-infant.com
- www.parent.net
- www.parenthub.com
- www.babycenter.com
- www.babiesonline.com

For Fathers

- www.fathermag.com
- www.newdads.com
- www.fatherhood.org
- www.divorcedfathers.com
- www.fathersnetwork.org
- www.fathers4kids.org
- www.mrdad.com

Immunizations

- www.immunizationinfo.org
- www.cdc.gov

Multiple Births

- www.tripletconnection.org
- www.twinsfoundation.com
- www.nomotc.org — National Organization of Mothers of Twins Clubs
- www.twinsadvice.com

Single Parent

- www.SingleParentTravel.net
- www.parentswithoutpartners.com
- www.divorcesupport.com

Disabilities

- www.childrenwithdiabetes.com
- www.aaaai.org - Information about allergies and asthma
- www.firstsigns.org - Information about early signs of autism
- www.parentcenterhub.org
- www.pave.org

Adoption

- www.adoptionnetwork.com
- www.adopt.org

Travel

- www.havechildrenwilltravel.com

Recalls

- www.recalls.gov

Toll-Free Numbers

National CDC Information Hotline	1-800-232-4636
La Leche League	1-800-525-3243
Nanny Care	1-800-383-5136
Child Care Association	1-800-543-7161
Lactation Hotline	1-877-452-5324
National Resource Center for Parents with Disabilities	1-800-644-2666
National Poison Center	1-800-222-1222
Consumer Product Safety Commission	1-800-638-2772
National Child Support Network, Inc.	1-800-729-5437
Au Pair in America	1-800-928-7247

Immunization Schedule

Vaccines	Birth	1 mo	2 mos	4 mos	6 mos	9 mos	12 mos	15 mos	18 mos	19-23 mos	2-3 yrs	4-6 yrs	7-10 yrs	11-12 yrs	13-15 yrs	16-18 yrs
Hepatitis B (HepB)	1st dose	2nd dose			3rd dose											
Rotavirus (RV) RV1 (2-dose series); RV5 (3-dose series)			1st dose	2nd dose												
Diptheria, tetanus, & acellular pertussis (DTaP :< 7yrs)			1st dose	2nd dose	3rd dose		4th dose					5th dose				
Tetanus, diphtheria, & acellular pertussis (Tdap: ≥7 yrs)														(Tdap)		
Haemophilus influenzae type b (Hib)			1st dose	2nd dose			3rd dose									
Pneumococcal conjugate (PCV13)			1st dose	2nd dose	3rd dose		4th dose									
Pneumococcal polysaccharide (PPSV23)																
Inactivated polio virus (IPV) (<18 yrs)			1st dose	2nd dose			3rd dose					4th dose				
Influenza (IIV; LAIV) 2 doses for some						Annual vaccination (IIV only)						Annual vaccination (IIV or LAIV)				
Measles, mumps, rubella (MMR)							1st dose					2nd dose				
Varicella (VAR)							1st dose					2nd dose				
Hepatitis A (HepA)							2-dose series									
Human papillomavirus (HPV2: females only; HPV4: males and females)														3-dose series		
Meningococcal (Hib-Men-CY≥6 weeks; MenACWY-D≥9 mos; MenACWY-CRM≥2 mos)														1st dose		Booster

Range of recommended ages for all children	Range of recommended ages for catch-up immunization	Range of recommended ages for certain high-risk groups	Range of recommended ages during which catch-up is encouraged and for certain high-risk groups	Not routinely recommended

(Source: American Academy of Pediatrics)

Developmental Steps Chart

*Approximate guidelines

2 TO 3 MONTHS	Smiles spontaneously Rolls over-Grasps rattle
6 MONTHS	Plays peek-a-boo Sits without support
9 MONTHS	Pulls to standing Knows mother or father
12 MONTHS	Walks Says five words
18 MONTHS	Follows two-to-three directions Walks up steps
24 MONTHS	Knows first and last name Pedals tricycle
36 MONTHS	Dresses with supervision Understands cold, tired, hungry

Development of Teeth Chart

Usual Time for Cutting Teeth

TOOTH	LOWER	OUR BABY	UPPER	OUR BABY
Central Incisor	6 to 8 Months		8 to 12 Months	
Lateral Incisor	8 to 12 Months		8 to 12 Months	
Canine (eye tooth)	8 to 20 Months		8 to 20 Months	
First Molar	12 to 15 Months		12 to 15 Months	
Second Molar	24 to 30 Months		24 to 30 Months	

First Dental Appointment: _____

Height and Weight Chart

AGE	WEIGHT	HEIGHT
1 MONTH		
2 MONTHS		
3 MONTHS		
4 MONTHS		
5 MONTHS		
6 MONTHS		
7 MONTHS		
8 MONTHS		
9 MONTHS		
10 MONTHS		
11 MONTHS		
12 MONTHS		
15 MONTHS		
18 MONTHS		
21 MONTHS		
24 MONTHS		
30 MONTHS		
36 MONTHS		
48 MONTHS		

Important 'Firsts'

SMILED _____

ROLLED OVER _____

REACHED FOR RATTLE _____

SAID MA-MA OR DA-DA _____

SAT UP WITHOUT SUPPORT_____

CRAWLED _____

PULLED UP _____

STOOD ALONE _____

FIRST WALKED WITH HELP _____

WALKED ALONE _____

CLIMBED STAIRS _____

SAID FIVE WORDS _____

COULD FEED WITH SPOON _____

COULD DRINK FROM A CUP_____

COULD RIDE A TRICYCLE _____

Snowy or Rainy Day Activities

For children ages 1 to 3

- ❏ Fingerplays (See Bibliography)
    - ❏ Eentsy, Weentsy Spider
    - ❏ Ten little Soldiers
    - ❏ I'm a little Teacup
- ❏ Finger painting-use non-toxic paints made just for this or can make your own.
- ❏ Blocks-building a fortress, a bridge, a castle or something else.

- ❏ Either small wood blocks or the large cardboard blocks are great.

- ❏ Blowing bubbles.

- ❏ Puzzles with big pieces. Wooden ones are best for little children.

- ❏ Play Dough or dough made from flour and water.

- ❏ Baking-helping with actual baking or pretend cooking on a miniature play stove.

- ❏ Stamps made from a potato haves and dipped in paint or on colored ink pads.

- ❏ Murals made on white shelf paper. All kinds of materials can be added to drawings.

- ❏ Collages made from magazine pictures or old wallpaper books.

- ❏ Masks or piñatas made with paper bags.

- ❏ Dress-up-A dress-up box is important to have. Thrift stores have many, inexpensive items for a dress-up box.

- ❏ Puppets made with old socks or small paper bags. A stage can be made from a cardboard box.

- ❏ A card table with a sheet over it makes a great tent.

- ❏ Music boxes

- ❏ Making fudge or taffy with a parent or childcare person.

- ❏ Good materials to have on hand for special activities are:

  - ❏ Toilet paper and paper towel tubes

  - ❏ Boxes of all shapes and sizes

  - ❏ Cotton

  - ❏ Used gift wrap papers

  - ❏ Egg cartons

  - ❏ Pieces of cardboard

❑ Pipe cleaners

❑ Stickers

❑ Plastic cookie cutters

❑ Paper plates

❑ Old greeting cards

❑ Felt or fabric scraps

❑ Old socks

❑ Old-fashioned clothes pins

❑ A big cardboard box makes a great playhouse if a parent can cut out a door and windows.

❑ Kids love having a special toy corner, drawer, or cupboard in the kitchen. They can be busy with their toys or old pots and pans, while a parent or childcare person is working in the kitchen. Be sure the special place is far away from the stove or a dangling coffee pot cord.

❑ A favorite indoor activity is having a small child lie down on a large sheet of plain white or brown paper and then drawing an outline of his or her body. The child can then color in the shape and add eyes, nose, mouth, or other features.

Activities for Children with Special Needs

Art

This is a wonderful creative outlet for any child but particularly for a special needs child.

Finger paints can help a child develop a good tactile sense and clay can help develop hand muscles and a three-dimensional sense. It is important to buy non-toxic clay that won't dry out.

Collages are fun to make and small pieces of paper, wood, material, beans, or pasta can be used. Magazine pictures can be used to make collages.

Brown paper bags can be used to make masks, puppets and even piñatas. Holiday themes can be used and all the art work should be displayed. As kids get older, art shows can be held for family members.

Games

Games with music can be fun and old-fashioned games such as London Bridge is Falling Down, Ring-a-Round-the Rosie, musical chairs, hide-and-seek and similar games can be adapted for kids depending on the child's disability.

Post office is fun for kids of all ages to play, as is banking, having a bakery, grocery store or being a doctor or nurse.

Toys

There are catalogues for special needs toys and the Internet can also be a source. Most little children need a stuffed animal to love and blocks are always a hit, unless a child has difficulty handling them.

Dress-up boxes can be a great source of fun and even kids in wheelchairs can enjoy playing dress-up. Thrift shops are a great source of old hats, scarves, gloves and other things to add to a dress-up box.

Chore Chart For Boys and Girls

AGE 2

❏ Dust

❏ Put away toys

❏ Help sweep with a child's broom

AGE 3

❏ Dusting

❏ Setting the table

❏ Emptying waste baskets

❏ Putting away toys

❏ Folding clothes

❏ Sweeping with a small broom

AGE 4

❏ Helping to make beds

❏ Sorting clothes

❏ Folding clothes

❏ Caring for pets

❏ Polishing silver

❏ Helping cook or bake

❏ Watering plants

Appendix III Medical & Special Needs Information

APGAR Scoring

This test was devised by Dr. Virginia Apgar and is the very first test given to a newborn. The test was developed to rapidly assess a newborn's physical condition and to see if extra medical or emergency care is needed. The score is recorded at one minute and then again at five minutes. Ten is a perfect score and a score in the lower range could be a cause of concern, but not necessarily. If the score is low, a third test may be given at 10 minutes.

	2	**1**	**0**
Heart Rate	Normal > 100/minute	< 100/minute	No pulse
Breathing	Normal	Slow or Irregular	No breathing
Responses	Moves with stimulation	Facial movement with stimulation	No response
Activity	Active	Little movement	None
Appearance	Normal color	Blue hands and feet	Pale all over

Medical Personnel You May Encounter

Pediatrician- A doctor who cares for children and teenagers. If they are members of the American Academy of Pediatrics, that means they are board-certified and have passed both oral and written examinations after their years of training. If they are board-qualified, the tests have not yet been passed.

Family Practice doctor-Sees both children and adults. If they are board-certified, they have completed the necessary years of training and passed specific tests.

Doctor of Osteopathy-D.O.-Has graduated from a college of osteopathy. Many apply for additional training in a medical school and then take exams to become M.D's.

Hospitalist-These are M.Ds who work just in hospitals. There are now both pediatric and adult hospitalists. Some doctors turn the hospital care of patients over to these doctors and don't visit their hospitalized patients.

Registered Nurse-R.N.-May have just nursing school training after high school. Others have a combined college and nursing school background.

Nurse Practitioner-N.P. This is an individual who has had further training after receiving an R.N. Some states allow them to see patients without a physician's supervision. They see patients in store mini-clinics. *These are not approved for children by the American Academy of Pediatrics.*

Physician Assistant-These individuals have a two year course of training and may or may not have a college degree. They work under a physician's supervision.

Signs and Symptoms of Common Childhood Diseases

Roseola Infantum (Exanthem Subitum)

This can be a frightening disease for parents. An infant or small child will have a high fever from one to five days with almost no other symptoms. Then the fever falls suddenly after the fourth or fifth day and a tiny, flat, small rash appears all over the body. The rash starts and is mostly seen on the baby's trunk. Some children are irritable and may have enlarged lymph nodes at the base of their skulls. The major complication is that convulsions or seizures can occur, if the temperature is not kept down by cooling measures and Tylenol. It is important for a child to be seen by a pediatrician or family doctor when the fever persists to be sure there are no other problems, as an ear infection, meningitis or other illness.

Chicken Pox (Varicella)

This childhood disease is very contagious with an **incubation period of 12 to 21days.** For the first twenty-four hours an infant or child may just have a slight fever, decreased appetite, and less energy. Then small red, blister-like spots or lesions are seen usually first on the trunk, then the chest, and back. The blisters come in bunches and cause quite severe itching. It is important to keep a child from scratching, so there will not be scarring or secondary infection. A child's fingernails should be kept short and cotton gloves or socks can be put over the hands. Antihistamines and cooling baths will help the itching. A child is contagious until the lesions have crusts on them. Encephalitis, an infection of the brain, is a rare complication, but should be watched for. Some mild cases of chicken pox are occurring despite immunization for this disease. However, the immunization is an important one for a child to receive.

Whooping Cough (Pertussis)

The **incubation period** for this disease **is seven to 10 days.** DPT immunization has prevented millions of cases. (D=diptheria, P= pertussis, and T= tetanus). However, as many parents refuse immunizations for their children, the number of cases is increasing. Initially, a child will have a cough, runny nose, and mild fever. In about two weeks, the cough will become severe and frequent with a "whoop" at the end of a cough. The coughing may last for several weeks. Antibiotics may help prevent secondary complications, but severe complications can occur. These can affect the lung causing pneumonia, or other problems. Convulsions and brain hemorrhage can also develop. Small infants should be closely watched and in a hospital.

Measles (Rubeola)

This disease has an **incubation period of eight to 14 days.** The first symptoms are usually fever, sore throat, cough, and runny nose. Red eyes (conjunctivitis) are a common accompanying symptom. The rash is usually seen about the fifth day and starts on the face, behind the ears, then goes to the chest, abdomen, and lastly the extremities. The rash gradually turns into large, red patches. Complications are ear infections, pneumonia, or encephalitis (an infection of the brain). A dark room may help because light often bothers a child's eyes. Itching can occur and can be treated with antihistamines or cool baths. A child should be kept as quiet as possible until there is no longer an elevated temperature.

Streptococcal Infections (Streptococcosis)

Group A streptococcus can cause severe disease if it is not recognized and treated. The **incubation period** for a strep throat infection (pharyngitis) is **two to five days.** A child will suddenly develop a fever; have a loss of appetite, red cheeks, and a severe sore throat. There may be white matter (exudate) on the tonsils, which can be quite large. There are usually big, boggy glands or lymph nodes under the chin at the angle of the jaw. A throat culture is important to have done prior to treatment with penicillin. A follow-up throat culture should be done after 10 days of treatment with penicillin to be sure the strep has been completely eliminated. Untreated strep throat can lead to kidney disease (glomerulonephritis), rheumatic fever, or scarlet fever. Ear infections may also occur.

Impetigo is a strep infection of the skin. The crusty, yellowish skin lesions are usually around the nose, ears, on the face, and shins. Other sites may also be infected. Treatment is cleansing frequently and antibiotics.

Mumps (Epidemic parotitis)

The **incubation period** for mumps is **12 to 24 days.** The onset is usually an elevated temperature followed by a loss of appetite and pain on chewing or behind the ears. Swelling occurs in the glands at the angle of the jaw extending to the face. A child should be kept in the house and quiet until the fever and swelling have subsided. A severe infection in the mouth or a tooth infection can mimic mumps. There are some serious complications of mumps, so the immunization is important for all children to receive.

Coxsackie and other viruses cause infections in children. These are quite common in the summer and fall months. The treatment is generally keeping the temperature under control, being sure enough liquids are taken and keeping a child as quiet as possible. This is important because otherwise, complications can occur.

Pneumococcal Disease

This is caused by the bacteria, Streptococcus pneumoniae. People with the disease can spread it by sneezing or coughing. Children with low resistance or chronic lung disease are at risk. Ear infections, sinusitis, pneumonia, eye infections, and meningitis can result in susceptible patients. Children under five years of age are particularly at risk.

Rotavirus Infection

Generally infants and children between the ages of three months and two years are the ones affected with this virus. The symptoms are diarrhea, fever, nausea, and vomiting. The most important thing is to be sure a child takes enough fluids to keep up with the diarrhea and the fever is kept under control. If a child is not urinating adequately and seems dehydrated, hospitalization may be necessary. It is important to keep in touch with the child's doctor during the illness. The incubation period is two to three days and the virus is very contagious. Usually the fever and vomiting will stop after two to three days, but the diarrhea may last for several more days. A stool culture may be necessary and a stool to look for ova and parasites. It would be important to be sure there is no accompanying ear infection.

Childhood Disabilities

Autism Spectrum Disorders

Autism, Asperger Syndrome, and Pervasive Developmental Disorder have all been lumped together now under the name Autism Spectrum Disorders. Autism is being diagnosed with increasing frequency and is more prevalent in boys than girls. The diagnosis can be made before the second year, but unfortunately few physicians have adequate training to do this or are hesitant to do so because they do not want to upset the parents. The typical signs of autism are considerable difficulty interacting with peers and usually lack of eye contact with others. Communicating may be difficult and speech can be absent or repetitive. Deafness may be present and hearing should always be checked in a pediatric hearing center. The children with ASD may be extremely bright, but some are developmentally delayed. Testing should be done by a qualified child psychologist. Asperger Syndrome is much less severe, but learning disabilities may be present and should be looked for.

Attention Deficit Disorder (ADHD)

Anxiety accompanies ADHD in twenty-five to fifty percent of children. Sitting still, focusing on tasks and difficulty with organization are common problems. Depression can also occur. Medication can be helpful, but should be carefully monitored.

Cerebral Palsy

There are three basic forms of cerebral palsy, and they can be due to injury at birth or the cause may be unknown. Some babies with cerebral palsy are quite floppy or hypotonic at birth and then develop increased tightness of the muscles or spasticity as they get older. A second form is writhing motions, called athetosis, with spasticity. The third form is marked spasticity in varying degrees throughout the body. There may be associated seizures and other problems. However, now injections of Botox has been found to be of some help with the spasticity and if just the lower extremities are involved surgical help is possible.

Congenital Myopathies

This is an important category of muscle disorders, unrecognized by many physicians, even some pediatric neurologists. The important of making a diagnosis of one of the myopathies in this group is that the muscle weakness improves with time in some and others have specific problems connected with them, which should be recognized. A condition called Malignant Hyperthermia is associated with the disorder called Central Core disease and if the wrong anesthetic is used during surgery, death can occur. The diagnosis, *congenital hypotonia,* is still being made by physicians and can even be found in medical textbooks. There is no such disorder, and a muscle biopsy and other tests should be done to find the exact diagnosis. A pediatric neuromuscular specialist should most likely be seen.

Deafness

Three out of 1,000 infants are found to be mildly or profoundly deaf. If a child is not saying words or babbling in the first three months and doesn't turn his or her head to sound, hearing should be checked at a pediatric hearing center. Cochlear implants can make a great difference in the life of a deaf child and should always be considered. Meningitis is a risk with these, but with good pediatric care, this should not prevent a child from having cochear implants and the ability to hear and speak.

Diabetes

When there is a family history of diabetes or the baby is extremely large, urinalysis and blood sugar tests can be done to be sure there is not a problem. The three symptoms of childhood diabetes, called Type one diabetes, are increased thirst, increased urination, and increased appetite. Weight loss and tiredness may also be present. Many doctors are not consistent about checking yearly urinalyses and these should always be done not only to look for diabetes, but to look for kidney disease or infection.

Duchenne Muscular Dystrophy

The diagnosis of this disorder can be made early, particularly if there is a family history. Two-thirds of the cases are genetic and the mothers carry the recessive gene. I have diagnosed children as early as eighteen months when there was not a family history. This can be done with a markedly elevated CPK blood test and muscle biopsy. Treatment should be started early because tightness of the muscles or contractures develop and these need stretching. Now small children should be routinely started on small doses of prednisone. There is still a debate about whether a dose needs to be given daily or can it be given every other day. It is important that weight gain and blood pressure be closely monitored. There is a treatable condition called **polymyositis** which can mimic Duchenne dystrophy. It may also have an elevated CPK. A muscle biopsy can show inflammation, but this can be negative in twenty-five percent of the cases. The rapid onset of muscle weakness is the principal clue to this disorder and prednisone treatment can return most children to normal muscle strength if the medication is started early and in an appropriate dose.

Heart Problems

Infants born with congenital heart disease should receive early diagnosis and treatment. Later on in childhood, a soft heart murmur may be heard. An experienced pediatrician or family doctor should be able to tell if a heart murmur is of concern and if there is ever a question a pediatric cardiologist should be consulted. Children born with Down Syndrome frequently have heart problems and surgery may be necessary early on.

Juvenile Rheumatoid Arthritis (JRA)

JRA can have an onset in early childhood, but may be hard to diagnosis because the laboratory tests may not be abnormal for some time. However, if a child, particularly a girl, has on-going pain in one joint a slit-lamp examination of the eyes by a pediatric ophthalmologist may make the diagnosis. This is particularly important because the eyes can be severely affected if not watched closely. Extreme pain at night in the hip or other joints can also a sign of JRA. A pediatric rheumatologist needs to be seen to make the diagnosis and start treatment.

Learning Disability

Learning disabilities can be passed down from a parent to a child. The diagnosis can be made by an experienced child psychologist who will do tests to determine if there is a problem. Special education help in the schools is available if the special education department of the school district is contacted. An IEP, or Individual Educational Plan, will be put together by a meeting of the parent or parents, the child's teacher, and any consultants, as a speech therapist. Each state has a specific number of days in which the special education office can respond to the request for help and an IEP. An early diagnosis is important, so a child can receive special help and not begin to dislike school or later, as a teenager, drop out. Two-thirds of prisoners are said to be learning disabled and most likely had little help or even a diagnosis.

Mental Illness

If a child is showing signs of abnormal or unusual behavior in the early years, it is important to find the best possible help. This would be a child psychologist to do some testing or play therapy and the help of a child psychiatrist may also be needed. Extreme anxiety, outbursts of rage, hurting other children or trying to destroy everything in sight are all signs of trouble. If a child does not receive professional help early on, serious long-term consequences can result. If your child's doctor says, *"Don't worry, your child will probably outgrow the problems,"* please don't listen, but take matters into your own hands. It is estimated that 21 percent of kids have a diagnosable mental illness, but just 1/5 sadly receive treatment. Sometimes this is due to the parents' denial and sometimes it is because they don't want their relatives and friends to know they have a child with a problem.

Needed Medical Supplies

❑ Rectal thermometer

❑ Vaseline to coat thermometer before inserting it.

❑ Rubbing alcohol to clean thermometer.

❑ Band-aides

❑ Phisohex or phisoderm for cleaning infected areas or cuts.

❑ Neosporin ointment for cuts.

❑ Gauze squares for larger cuts or burns.

❑ Cool mist vaporizer for croup or stuffy noses.

❑ Sunscreen for babies older than six months for outdoors on hot days.

❑ Tylenol drops or liquid.

Resources for Special Needs Kids

Alaska

Health Care Program for Children
with Special Needs
3601 C Street
Suite 902
Anchorage, AK 99503
1-888-268-4632

American Samoa

Maternal & Child Health & Crippled
Children's Program
LBJ Tropical Medical Center
Division of Public Health
Pago Pago, American Samoa 96799
1-664-633-4686

Arkansas

Children's Medical Services
Department of Human Services
P.O. Box 1437a
Slot 526
Little Rock, AR 72203
1-800-482-5850

California

Children's Medical Services Branch
714 "P" St., Room 350
Sacramento, CA 95814
1-916-445-4171

Colorado

Health Care Program for Children
with Special Needs

Colorado Department of Health
4300 Cherry Creek Dr. South
Denver, CO 80222
1-303-692-2370

Connecticut

Children with Special Health Care
Needs
Department of Health
410 Capital Street
P. O. Box 340308
Hartford, CT 06134
1-860-509-8074

District of Colombia

Health Services for Children with
Special Needs
State Department of Human Services
1101 Vermont Ave.
Twelfth floor
Washington, DC 20005
1-202-467-2737
1-866-937-4549

Florida

Children's Medical Services Program
Department of Health and
Rehabilitation Services
4052 Bald Cypress Way
Bin A 13
Tallahassee, FL 32399
1-850-245-4465

Georgia

Children's Medical Services
Department of Human Resources
Two Peachtree Street
Eleventh Floor N.W.
Atlanta, GA 30303
1-404-657-2726

Idaho

Children's Special Health Program
Department of Health and Welfare
PTC Bldg.
Fourth Floor
P.O. Box 83720
Boise, ID 83720-0036
1-877-887-3075

Illinois

Division of Specialized Care
for Children
570 Devonshire
Suite A
Champaign, IL 61820-7306
1-800-779-0880
Fax: 1-217-244-4212

Indiana

Children's Special Health
Care Services
Indiana State Department of Health
Two North Meridian Street
Section C
Indianapolis, IN 46206
1-800-475-1555
1-317-233-1351

Iowa

Child Health Specialty Clinic
University of Iowa
247 Hospital School
Iowa City, IA 52242
1-319-356-1616

Kansas

Services for Children with Special
Health Care Needs
State Department of Health
and Environment
1000 S.W. Jackson
Topeka, KS 66612
1-785-296-1086

Kentucky

Commission for Children with
Special Health Care Needs
1600 Breckenridge Street
Owensboro, KY. 42303
1-270-687-7038

Louisiana

Children's Special Health Services
Department of Health and Hospitals
Office of Public Health
P.O. Box 60630
Room 607
New Orleans, LA 70160
1-504-568-5055

Maine

Bureau of Children with
Special Needs

Department of Mental Health and
Mental Retardation
State House, Station No. 40
Augusta, ME 04333
1-207-624-9494

Maryland
Children's Medical Services
Department of Mental Health
201 W. Preston Street
Room 423A
Baltimore, MD 21201
1-800-638-8864

Massachusetts
Division for Children with Special
Health Needs
Bureau of Family and
Community Health
One Ashburton Place
Eleventh Floor
150 Tremont St.
Boston, MA 02108
1-617-573-1600

Michigan
Children's Special Health
Care Services
Department of Public Health
Capitol View Bldg.
201 Townsend Street
Lansing, MI 48913
1-517-373-3740

Minnesota
Minnesota Children with Special
Health Needs
Division of Family Services
Department of Health
717 Delaware St. S.E.
P.O. Box 9441
Minneapolis, MN 55440
1-651-201-3650

Missouri
Bureau of Special Health Care Needs
Department of Health
P.O. Box 570
Jefferson City, MO 65102-0570
1-314-751-6246

Montana
Children with Special Health Needs
Bureau of Maternal and Child Health
P.O. Box 202951
Helena, MT 59620-2051
1-406-444-3622
Fax: 1-406-444-2750

Nebraska
Medically Handicapped
Children's Program
Department of Social Services
301 Centennial Mall South
Lincoln, NE 68509
1-402-471-3121

New Hampshire
Bureau of Special Medical Services

Office of Family and
Community Health
Division of Public Health Services
129 Pleasant Street
Concord, NH 03301-3852
603-271-4440
1-800-852-3345 (in New Hampshire)
Fax: 1-603-271-4729

New Jersey
Special Child Health Services
Department of Health, CN 634
Trenton, NJ 08625
1-609-292-5676

New Mexico
Children's Medical Services
State Department of Health
1190 South St. Francis Street
Santa Fe, NM 87502
1-505-841-6100
1-800-797-3260

New York
Physically Handicapped
Children's Services
Bureau of Child and
Adolescent Health
Corning Tower Bldg.
Room 208
Empire State Plaza
Albany, NY 12237
1-518-474-2001

North Carolina
Children's Special Health Services
Department of Environment, Health,
and Natural Resources
P.O. Box 29597
Raleigh, N.C. 2726-0597
1-919-715-3812
1-800-737-3028

North Dakota
Children's Special Health Services
Department of Human Services
State Capitol
600 E. Boulevard Ave.
Bismarck, ND 58505
1-701-328-2436

Oklahoma
Children with Special Health
Care Needs
State Department of Human Services
P.O.Box 25352
Oklahoma City, OK 73125
1-405-521-3679
1-866-411-1877
Fax: 1-405-521-4158

Pennsylvania
Division of Children's Special Health
Care Needs
Bureau of Maternal and Child
Preventative Health
State Department of Health
625 Forfter Street
Harrisburg, PA 17120

1-877-724-3258
Fax: 1-717-772-0323

Puerto Rico
Children with Special Health Needs
P. O. Box 70184
Puerto Nuevo, PR 00921
1-787-274-5660
1-800-981-5721
Fax: 787-274-3301

Rhode Island
Office of Special Needs
Department of Education
Roger Williams Bldg., Rm. 209
22 Hayes St.
Providence, RI 02908
1-401-444-5685

South Carolina
Children's Rehabilitative Services
Division of Children with Special
Health Care Needs
Department of Health and
Environment Control
Mills Jarrett Complex
P. O. Box 101106
Columbia, SC 29211
1-803-898-0784
1-800-868-0404

South Dakota
Children's Special Health Services
Department of Health
445 E. Capital

Pierre, SD 57501
1-605-773-3737

Tennessee
Children's Special Services
Department of Health
Cordell Hull Bldg.
Fifth Floor
425 Fifth Ave. North
Nashville, TN 37243
1-615-741-0361
Fax: 1-615-741-1063

Texas
Children's Health Division
Texas Department of Health
P.O. Box 13247
Austin, TX 78711-3247
1-800-252-5400
Fax: 1-888-780-8099

Utah
Children with Special Health
Care Needs
Community and Family
Health Services
Department of Health
P.O. Box 141010
44 No. Medical Dr.
Salt Lake City, UT 84114-1010
1-801-538-6003

Vermont
Children with Special Health
Care Needs

Department of Health
108 Cherry St.
Burlington, VT 05401
1-802-863-7338

(U.S.) Virgin Islands

Services for Children with Special
Health Care Needs
Division of Maternal and
Child Health
Department of Health
3500 Estate Richmond
Christiansted
St. Croix, VI 00820
1-340-773-1311

Virginia

Children's Specialty Services
Virginia Department of Health
109 Governor Drive
Eighth Floor
Richmond, VA 23219
1-804-864-7706

Washington

Children with Special Health
Care Needs
River View Corporate Center
Suite 1500
16201 East Indiana Ave.
Spokane Valley, WA 99216
1-800-525-0127

West Virginia

Handicapped Children's Services
Office of Maternal and Child Health
Bureau of Public Health
350 Capitol Street
Charleston, WV 25301
1-304-558-5388

Wisconsin

Program for Children with Special
Health Care Needs
Department of Health and
Social Services
1000 Lake View Drive
Wausau, WI 54401
1-715-261-1906

Wyoming

Children's Health Services
6101 Yellowstone Road Suite 420
Cheyenne, WY 82002
1-307-777-6921
1-800-438-5795
Fax: 1-307-777-7215

Appendix IV
Helpful Information

Resources for Parents

Child Care

Child Care Aware
1515 North Courthouse Road
Eleventh Floor
Arlington, VA 22201
www.naccara.org

National Child Care Association
2025 M Street NW Suite 800
Washington D C., 20036-3309
1-800-543-7161

Child Care, Inc.
322 Eighth Ave
New York, NY 10001
1-212-929-4999

Au Pair in America
River Plaza
9 W. Broad Street
Stamford, CT 06902
1-800-928-7247
www.aupairinamerica.com

National Head
Start Association
1651 Prince Street
Alexandria, VA 22314
1-703-739-0875
www.nhsa.org

Zero To Three-National Center
for Infants, Toddlers, and
Families
2000 M Street NW Suite 200
Washington D C 20036
1-800-899-4301
www.zerotothree.org

International Nanny Association
2020 Southwest Freeway Suite 208
Houston, TX 77098
1-888-878-1477
www.nanny.org

Child Safety

National Safe Kids Campaign

1301 Pennsylvania Ave. N.W.
Suite 1000
Washington D.C. 2004-1707
1-202-662-0600
www.safekids.org

Health Issues

American Academy
of Pediatrics
141 Northwest Point Blvd.
P.O. Box 927
Elkgrove Village, IL 60009-0927
1-866-843-2271
www.aap.org

Asthma and Allergy Foundation
8201 Corporate Drive Suite 1000
Landover, MD 20785
www.aafa.org

Marriage and Relationships

American Association for
Marriage and Family Therapy
112 S. Alfred St.
Alexandria, VA 22314
1-703-838-9808
www.aamft.org

Parent Care, Inc.
For parents who have lost a child
1-919-350-8567

American Association of
Premature Infants (A.A.P.I.)
P.O. Box 6920
Cincinnati, OH 45206
www.aapi-online.org

National Perinatal Association
2090 Linglestown Rd.
Hamsburg, PA 17110
www.nationalperinatal.org

Step-parents

Stepfamily Foundation, Inc.
333. W. End Ave.
New York, NY 10023
www.stepfamily.org

Special Needs

Autism Society of America
7910 Woodmont Ave. Suite 650
Bethesda, MD 20814
1-800-328-8476
www.autism-society.org

Arthritis Foundation
1314 Spring Street N.W.
Atlanta, GA 30309
1-404-872-7100

Celiac Disease Foundation
13251 Ventura Suite One
Studio City, CA 91604
www.celiac.org

National Down
Syndrome Congress
30 Mansell Court Suite 108
Roswell, GA 30076
1-800-232-6372

Federation for Children with
Special Needs
1135 Tremont Street Suite 420
Boston, MA 02120
1-800-331-0688 (in MA)
www.fcsn.org

National Autism Hotline
P.O. Box 507
605 Ninth Ave.
Huntington, WV 25710
1-800-422-4453
www.nationalautismassociation.org

United Cerebral Palsy
1660 L. Street NW Suite 700
Washington, DC 20036
1-800-872-5827
www.ucpa.org

Single Parents

Parents Without Partners
1560 S. Dixie Hwy Suite 510
Boca Raton, FL 33432

www.parentswithoutpartners.org

State Child Care Resources

Alabama
Child Care Services Division
Department of Human Resources
50 North Ripley Street
Montgomery, AL 36130
1-334-242-1425
1-866-528-1694
Fax: 1-334-353-1491
www.alabama.gov/services/child

Alaska
Department of Health and
Social Services
Division of Public Assistance
Child Care Programs Office
3601 C Street, Suite 14
Anchorage, AK 99524
1-888-268-4632
Fax: 1-907-269-4635
**www.hss.state.ak.us/dpa/
programs/ccare**

Arizona
Department of Economic Security
Child Care Administration
315 West Fort Lowell Road
Tucson, AZ 85705
1-520-293-0214
www.azdes.gov/childcare

Arkansas

Department of Human Services
Division of Child Care
700 Main Street
Little Rock, AR 72203-1437
1-501-682-6590
1-800-445-3316
Fax: 1-501-583-2327
www.arkansas.gov/childcare

California

Department of Education
Child Development Division
1430 N Street, Suite 3410
Sacramento, CA 95814-5901
1-916-322-6233
Fax: 1-916-323-6853
www.cde.ca.gov/sp/cd

Commonwealth of the Northern Mariana Islands

CNMI Public School System
P.O. Box 501370
Saipan, MP 96950
1-670-237-3028
www.cnmipss.org

Connecticut

Department of Social Services
Family Services Unit
55 Farmington Ave.,
Hartford, CT 06106-3730
1-855-626-6632

1-800-811-6141 (within state)
Fax: 1-860-424-5335
www.dss.state.ct.us/ccare

Delaware

Health and Social Services
Division of Social Services
P.O. Box 906, Lewis Building
1901 N. DuPont Highway
New Castle, DE 19720-1100
1-302-255-9643
1-800-372-2022
Fax: 1-302-255-4425

District of Columbia

Early Care and
Education Administration
825 North Capitol Street N.E.
Second Floor
Washington D.C. 20002
1-202-442-5888 or 1-202-442-5929
Fax: 1-202-442-9430

Florida

Agency for Workforce Innovation
Office of Early Learning
230 Marriott Drive
Caldwell Building
Tallahassee, FL 32399-4120
1-850-717-8550
www.floridajobs.org/earlylearning/index.html

Georgia

Department of Human Resources
Division of Family and
Children Services
Child Care Unit
Two Peachtree Street NW, Suite
21-293
Atlanta, GA 30303-3142
1-404-657-3441
Fax: 1-404-657-4389
www.div.dhr.state.ga.us/dfcs

Guam

Department of Public Health and
Social Services
Division of Public Welfare-CCDF
P.O. Box 2816
Hagatna, GU 96932
1-671-735-7274
Fax: 1-671-734-7015

Hawaii

Department of Human Services
Benefit, Employment and
Support Services
1390 Miller Street Room 209
P. O. Box 339
Honolulu, HI 96813
1-808-586-7050
Fax: 1-808-586-4884
www.state.hi.us/dhs

Idaho

Department of Health and Welfare,
Benefit Program Operations
P.O. Box 83720
Boise, ID 83720-0036
1-208-334-5656
Fax: 1-208-334-4916
www.idahochild.org

Illinois

Department of Human Services
Office of Child Care Services
400 West Lawrence, 3rd Floor
Springfield, IL 62762-0001
1-217-785-2559
Fax: 1-217-524-6030
www.dhs.state.il.us/ts/

Indiana

Family and Social Services
Administration
Division of Family Resources
402 W. Washington Street, W-392
Indianapolis, IN 46204
1-317-234-3313
1-800-441-7837
Fax: 1-317-233-6093
www.in.gov/fssa/children/bcd

Iowa

Department of Human Services
Bureau of Family and
Community Services
Hoover State Office Building

1305 E. Walnut, Div. of
BDPS-Fifth Floor
Des Moines, IA 50319-0114
1-515-281-7272
Fax: 1-515-242-6036
**www.dhs.state.is.us/dhs2005/dhs.
homepage/childrenfamily/childcare/
index.html**

Kansas

Department of Social and
Rehabilitation Services
Docking State Office Building
915 SW Harrison, 681W
Topeka, KS 66612
1-785-826-8000
Fax: 1-785-368-8159
**www.srskansas.org/ISD/ees/
child_care.htm**

Kentucky

Cabinet for Health and
Family Services
Division of Child Care
275 East Main St., 3W-B
Frankfort, KY 40621
1-502-564-2524
1-800-421-1903
Fax: 1-502-564-3464
**www.cfc.state.ky.us/help/Child
Care.asp**

Louisiana

Division of Child Care and Early
Childhood Education
Department of Social Services
Office of Family Support
627 North Fourth Street
Baton Rouge, LA 70802
1-800-256-4650
Fax: 1-225-219-4248
**www.dss.state.la.us/departments/
ofs/Child_Care_Assistance_
Program.html**

Maine

Department of Health and
Human Services
Office of Child Care and Head Start
11 State House Station
Marquardt Bldg.
Augusta, ME 04333-0011
1-207-624-7509
Fax: 1-207-287-6156
**www.maine.gov/dhhs/occhs/index.
htm**

Maryland

Department of Education
Division of Early
Childhood Development
Office of Child Care
200 West Baltimore Street
Baltimore, MD 21201
1-410-767-7128
1-800-332-6347

Fax: 1-410-333-8699
**www.marylandpublicschools.org/
msde**

Massachusetts
Department of Early Education
and Care
600 Washington Street, Suite 6100
Boston, MA 02111
1-617-988-6600
Fax: 1-617-988-2451
www.eec.state.ma.us/

Michigan
Department of Human Services
Child Development and
Care Division
235 South Grand Ave., Suite 1302
P.O. Box 30037
Lansing, MI 48909-7537
1-517-241-0669
Fax: 1-517-335-6236
www.michigan.gov/dhs

Minnesota
Department of Human Services
Child Care Assistance Program
P.O. Box 64266
St. Paul, MN 55164
1-651-431-3809
Fax: 1-651-431-7528
www.dhs.state.mn.us

Mississippi
Department of Human Services

Office for Children and Youth
750 North State Street
Jackson, MS 39202
1-601-359-4555
1-800-877-7882
Fax: 1-601-359-4422
www.mdhs.state.ms.us/ocy.html

Missouri
Department of Social Services
Children's Division, Office of
Early Childhood
P.O. Box 88
Jefferson City, MO 65102
1-573-751-6793
Fax: 1-573-526-9586
www.dss.mo.gov/cd/childcare

Montana
Department of Public Health
Human and Community
Services Division
P.O. Box 202952
Helena, MT 59620-2952
1-406-444-1828
Fax: 1-406-444-2547
www.dphhs.mt.gov

Nebraska
Department of Health and
Human Services
Child Care
P.O. Box 95026
Lincoln, NE 68509

1-402-471-9272

Fax: 1-402-471-9597

www.hhs.state.ne.us/chs/chc/
chcindex.htm

Nevada

Department of Human Resources

Welfare Division

1100 East William Street

Suite 101

Carson, City NV 89701

1-775-684-3676

Fax: 1-775-684-0617

www.welfare.state.nv.us/welfare,htm

New Hampshire

Department of Health and

Human Services

Division for Children, Youth &

Families, Child Development Bureau

129 Pleasant Street

Concord, NH 03301-3857

1-603-271-8153

Fax: 1-603-271-4729

www.dhhs.state.nh.us/DHHS/CDB/
default.htm

New Jersey

Department of Human Services

Division of Family Development

6 Quakerbridge plaza

P.O.Box 716

Trenton, NJ 08625-0716

1-609-588-2163

1-800-332-9227

Fax: 1-609-588-3051

www.state.nj.us/humanservices/

New Mexico

Children, Youth and

Families Department

Child Care Services Bureau

P.E.R.A. Building, Room 121

P.O. Drawer 5160

Santa Fe, NM 87502-5160

1-505-476-0465:

1-800-832-1321

Fax: 1-505-827-7361

www.newmexicokids.org

New York

Department of Family Assistance

Office of Children and Family Services

Bureau of Early Childhood Services

52 Washington St., Room 338,

North Bldg.

Rensselaer, NY 12144

1-518-474-9454

Fax: 1-518-474-9617

www.dfa.state.ny.us

North Carolina

Department of Health and

Human Services

Division of Child Development

2201 Mail Service Center

Raleigh, NC 27699-2201

1-919-527-6335

Fax: 1-919-715-1012

www.ncchildcare.dhhs.state.nc.us/ general/home.asp

North Dakota

Department of Human Services
Children and Family Services Division
State Capitol
600 E. Boulevard Ave.
Bismarck. ND 58505-0250
1-701-328-1725
1-800-755-2716 (In state)
Fax: 1-701-328-3538
www.state.nd.us/humanservices/ services/financialhelp/childcare. html

Ohio

Department of Job and
Family Services
Bureau of Child Care
and Development
2706 Airport Drive Suite 160
Columbus, Ohio 43211
1-614-395-5959
1-877-547-5978
Fax: 1-614-728-6803
www.jfs.ohio.gov

Oklahoma

Department of Human Services
Division of Child Care
P.O. Box 25352
Oklahoma City, OK 73125-0352

1-405-521-3561
1-800-347-2276
Fax: 1-405-522-2564
www.okdhs.org

Oregon

Department of Employment
Child Care Division
P.O. Box 14050
Salem, OR 97309-4050
1-503-947-1400
1-800-556-6616
Fax: 1-503-947-1428

Pennsylvania

Department of Public Welfare
Office of Child Development
Room 521, Health and Welfare Bldg.
Harrisburg, PA 17105-2675
1-717-346-9330
1-800-966-KIDS
1-877-4-PA-KIDS (Within state)
www.dpw.state.pa.us/Child/ childcare

Puerto Rico

Administration of Integral Child Care
and Development
Constitution Avenue, Stop 2
P.O. Box 15091
San Juan, PR 00902-5091
1-787-765-2929
Fax: 1-787-723-5357

Rhode Island

Department of Human Services
Office of Child Care
206 Elmwood Avenue
Providence, RI 02907
1-401-415-8396
Fax: 1-401-415-8226
**www.dhs.ri.gov/dhs/famchild/
dcspgm.htm**

South Carolina

Department of Social Services
Division of Child Care Services
P.O. Box 5616
Greenville, S.C. 29606
1-864-250-8297
1-800-768-5858 (In state)
Fax: 1-803-898-7625
**www.state.sc.dss/childcare/index.
html**

South Dakota

Department of Social Services
Division of Child Care Services
700 Governors Drive
Pierre, SD 57501-2291
1-605-773-4766
1-800-227-3020
Fax: 1-605-773-7294
**www.state.sd.us/social/ccs/ccshome.
htm**

Tennessee

Department of Human Services

Child Care, Adult and
Community Programs
400 Deaderick Street
Nashville, TN 37248-9600
1-615-313-5000
Fax: 1-615-532-9956
**www.state.tn.us/humanserv/
childcare.htm**

Texas

Workforce Commission
Child Care Services
P. O. Box 13247
Austin, TX 78711-3247
1-800-252-5400
Fax: 1-888-780-8099
**www.twc.state.tx.us/svcs/childcare/
ccinfo.html**

Utah

Department of Health
P .O. Box 14010
Salt Lake City, UT 84114-1010
1-801-538-6003
Fax: 1-801-526-4349
www.jobs.utah.gov/occ

Vermont

Department for Children and Families
Child Development Division
103 South Main Street
Two and Three North
Waterbury, VT 05671-5500
1-800-649-2642

Fax: 1-802-649-3642
www.dcf.state.vt.us/cdd

Virginia

Department of Social Services
Division of Child Care
and Development
Office of Child Care
2001 Maywill Street Suite 104
Richmond, VA 23230
1-800-552-3431
Fax: 1-804-36785420
**www.dss.virginia.gov/family/cc/
index.html**

Virgin Islands

Department of Human Services
Knud Hansen Complex-Bldg.A
1303 Hospital Ground
St. Thomas, VI 00802
1-340-774-0930
Fax: 1-340-774-3466

Washington

Depart of Social Services
Division of Child Care and
Early Learning
P. O. Box 45010
Olympia, WA 98504-5010
1-360-725-4665
1-866-482-4325
Fax: 1-360-413-3482
www1.dshs.wa.gov/esa/dcce

West Virginia

Department of Health and
Human Resources
Division of early Care and Education
1701 Fifth Avenue Box Four
Charleston, WV 25387
1-888-595-8290
Fax: 1-304-55414-4694
www.wvdhhr,org/bef

Wisconsin

Department of
Workforce Development
Child Care Section
201 East Washington Ave.
P. O. Box 7972
Madison, WI 53707-7972
1-608-266-3443
1-888-713-5437
Fax: 1-608-261-6968
**www.dwd.state.wi.us/dws/program/
childcare/default.htm**

Wyoming

Department of Family Services
Hathaway Building
Third Floor
2300 Capitol Avenue
Cheyenne, WY 82002-0490
1-307-777-7561
1-307-777-7747
www.dfsweb.state.wy.us/

Bibliography

Adams, Jerry. *How to Raise Disciplined and Happy Children.* CreateSpace, Charleston, S.C. 2011

Carroll, Deborah, Stella Rend. *Nanny 911.* HarperCollins, New York. 2005

Cole, Joanna, Stephanie Calmenson. *The Eentsy, Weentsy Spider Fingerplays and Action Rhymes.* Mulberry Books, New York. 1991.

Conner, Bobbi. *Unplugged Play.* Workman, New York. 2007.

Conner, Bobbi. *Everyday Opportunities for Extraordinary Parenting.* Sourcebooks, Naperville, Il. 2000.

Conner, Bobbi. *The Parent's Journal Guide to Raising Great Kids.* Bantam Books, New York, NY. 1997.

Conner, Bobbi. *The Giant Book of Creativity for Kids.* Roost Books, Boston, MA. 2015

Eiger, Marvin, Sally Wendkos Olds. *The Complete Book of Breast Feeding.* Workman, New York. 1999.

Eisen, Andrew, Linda Engler. *Helping Your Child Overcome Separation Anxiety or School Refusal.* New Harbinger Pub, Inc. Oakland, CA 2006.

Ellison, Sheila, Barbara Bennett. *365 Ways To Raise Confident Kids.* Sourcebooks, Inc. Naperville, IL. 2006.

Ferro, Pamela. *The Everything Twins, Triplets & More Books.* Adams Media, Avon, MA. 2005.

Greenberg, Gary, Jeannie Hayden. *A Practical Handbook for New Dads.* Simon and Schuster, New York, NY. 2004.

Karp, Harvey M.D. *The Happiest Baby Guide to Great Sleep.* William Morrow, New York, NY. 2013.

Lansky, Vicki. *Games Babies Play.* Book Peddlers, Minnetonka, MN 2001.

Linden Dana, Emma Paroli, Mia Doron. *Preemies.* Pocket Books, New York. 2000.

Neifert, Marianne, M.D. *The Essential Guide to Breastfeeding.* Sterling, New York, NY 2009.

Priwer, Shana, Cynthia Phillips. *The Everything Cooking for Baby and Toddler Book.* Adams Media, Avon, MA 2006.

Thompson, Charlotte. *Raising a Handicapped Child.* Oxford University Press, New York. 2000.

Thompson, Charlotte. *Raising a Child with a Neuromuscular Disorder.* Oxford University Press, New York. 1999.

Thompson, Charlotte. *101 Ways To The Best Medical Care.* Infinity Publishers, West Conshohocken, PA. 2006.

Weissbluth, Marc. *Healthy Habits, Happy Child.* Ballantine, New York. 2003

Wolraich, Mark, Sherill Tippins. *Guide to Toilet Training.* BantamDel, New York. 2003

Author Biography

 Charlotte E. Thompson, M.D. has been a practicing pediatrician for fifty years. She holds a B.A. and M.D. from Stanford University, is a Fellow of the American Academy of Pediatrics and an Assistant Clinical Professor of Pediatrics at U C San Diego Medical School. In 2005 and 2007, she was named as one of the Top Pediatricians in the United States by the Consumer's Research Council of America.

Dr. Thompson is a mother, a grandmother, and the author of eight books including *Raising a Handicapped Child* published in 1986, and now in its fifth edition.

Index